EVERYONE DESERVES A *GREAT* MANAGER

THE 6 CRITICAL PRACTICES FOR LEADING A TEAM

SCOTT MILLER WITH
TODD DAVIS AND VICTORIA ROOS OLSSON

SIMON &
SCHUSTER

London · New York · Sydney · Toronto · New Delhi

A CBS COMPANY

First published in the United States by Simon & Schuster, Inc., 2019
First published in Great Britain by Simon & Schuster UK Ltd, 2019
A CBS COMPANY

Copyright © Franklin Covey Co., 2019

1 3 5 7 9 10 8 6 4 2

Simon & Schuster UK Ltd
1st Floor
222 Gray's Inn Road
London WC1X 8HB

www.simonandschuster.co.uk
www.simonandschuster.com.au
www.simonandschuster.co.in

Simon & Schuster Australia, Sydney
Simon & Schuster India, New Delhi

A CIP catalogue record for this book is available from the British Library.

Trade Paperback ISBN: 978-1-4711-8191-7
eBook ISBN: 978-1-4711-8192-4

Printed in the UK by CPI Group (UK) Ltd, Croydon, CR0 4YY

MIX
Paper from
responsible sources
FSC
www.fsc.org   FSC® C020471

CONTENTS

FOREWORD

Want a guaranteed conversation starter? Ask someone if they've ever had a bad manager. And then brace yourself, because almost all of us know what it's like to work for a soul-crushing, morale-killing, please-don't-make-me-go-to-work kind of manager.

But if we're fortunate, we've also worked with a great manager—one who cared about us, believed in us, and helped us do our best work.

Legendary Harvard Business School professor Clayton Christensen believes management is one of the most meaningful roles in the world. In *How Will You Measure Your Life?* he writes, "If you want to help other people, be a manager. If done well, management is among the most noble of professions. You are in a position where you have eight or ten hours every day from every person who works for you. You have the opportunity to frame each person's work so that, at the end of every day, your employees will go home . . . living a life filled with motivators."

And the data proves it. According to Gallup, "Managers account for at least 70% of variance in employee engagement scores across business units."[*]

Being a great manager is one of the most influential roles—and one of the hardest. When I led a team for the first time, I struggled to learn on the job. What I wouldn't have given for a Wikipedia for managers, or even better, a WebMD for my leadership aches and pains. It didn't exist; so my cofounder and I set out to create one in a drafty San Francisco basement eight years ago.

The resulting company, Jhana, was founded on the idea that everyone deserves a great manager. (While there are impassioned arguments

---

[*] Gallup, Inc. (n.d.). Managers Account for 70% of Variance in Employee Engagement. Retrieved from https://news.gallup.com/businessjournal/182792/managers-account -variance-employee-engagement.aspx.

around the terms "leader" and "manager," the authors and I will use them interchangeably in this book for ease of reading.) Jhana now serves as an online learning resource that provides bite-size training for leaders, and our research confirmed how universally hard it was to transition into leadership, how often new managers weren't set up for success, and how little direction they received from their bosses. Our team of PhDs, researchers, writers, and technologists dove into the academic research and built a panel of managers to validate or refute their findings in the real world. What emerged was some of the best, most practical solutions for the challenges all managers face: delegating, leading people, setting the right goals, supporting people, hiring, firing, and motivating.

Apparently, I wasn't the only new manager who could use the help, because Jhana took off. Managers used our practical solutions in tech companies, professional services, financial services, hospitals, manufacturing, schools, universities, and governments. To increase our impact, we joined up with FranklinCovey, one of the most respected leadership-development companies in the world. Beginning with its cofounder, Dr. Stephen R. Covey, author of *The 7 Habits of Highly Effective People*, FranklinCovey has nearly four decades of experience around these fundamental leadership issues:

- How could we help people make one of the most difficult transitions of their careers, from individual contributor to manager, giving them the confidence to overcome their self-doubt?

- How could we help managers fulfill their potential and continue to learn and develop over time?

- How could we help them manage the often crushing stress that comes with the job?

With FranklinCovey's principle-based leadership legacy and Jhana's innovative Silicon Valley approach, we built a leadership solution that combined the best of both worlds: the 6 Critical Practices for Leading a Team, used by hundreds of thousands of managers in countries all over the world.

Although created primarily for managers leading teams of individual contributors, the practices in this book apply to leaders at any level:

If you're a new manager: You'll uncover the proven best practices to lead and develop your people into a high-performing team.

If you're an experienced manager: Focus on the practices that fill the gaps in your management training, and check out the tools for your most critical interactions such as conducting 1-on-1s, setting goals, and leading through change.

If you're a leader of leaders: You'll find practical ways to sharpen your managerial skills. This book can also serve as a guide to mentor new managers who report to you.

If you're a human resource, learning and development, or organizational development professional: Use this book to coach experienced managers and develop new/emerging leaders.

If you're a C-level executive: Use this book to model the practices so they manifest on the front line. If you're not using these practices, your managers probably won't either.

Along with Scott, Todd, and Victoria, I have found leadership to be especially challenging but also very rewarding. But if you're not there yet, the practices in this book will help you get there. Enjoy this journey that will inspire managers at any level to make an impact with their teams and leave a lasting legacy.

—*Rob Cahill*
Cofounder and CEO, Jhana
Vice President, FranklinCovey

EVERYONE DESERVES A GREAT MANAGER

INTRODUCTION

I hate powdered sugar.

It all started when I was twenty-seven years old, and three months into my new career with the Covey Leadership Center (what would become FranklinCovey) as a frontline salesperson for K–12 schools. After an entire life in Florida, including four years with the Walt Disney Company, I was excited about my new start in Utah, with its wide-open career opportunities and delightful absence of parking-lot alligators. Imagine my surprise when the vice president asked if I would take on the additional role of managing a team of client-service coordinators.

All of the people on the team had been with the company longer than me. Surveying my new team, I rendered my judgment: they were quite capable, but in need of motivation, accountability, and a young but promising leader who could raise the bar on performance.

I buckled down and got to the job at hand. The vice president was going to be thrilled with the outcomes I was able to produce. My team would revere my inspiring style and expertise. I was going to be so effective that it would be only a matter of time before I landed another promotion, a raise, and an even larger team to lead toward greatness.

That's not quite what happened.

Trying to increase productivity and our results, I suddenly found myself monitoring arrival and departure times. I banned personal appointments during work hours. I even asked a coordinator to respond to voicemails and report any issues to me while she was out of the office—*on her honeymoon.*

She thought I was joking.

I was not.

(To her credit, she flat-out refused. We are good friends to this day, twenty-two years later.)

So yes, I was quite effective—at destroying morale, people's self-

•

esteem, and any shred of pride they had in their work. I was tyrannical. I was a nightmare. Fine: I was a total jackass. But I genuinely thought my brand of swagger would bring everyone in line and inspire them to new levels of engagement.

Which brings us to the powdered sugar. One morning during my reign of terror, I was reading the paper at a local diner before work while (you guessed it) eating a waffle with powdered sugar on top, when my phone rang. It was the vice president. Time for my next promotion!

Instead, he began with, "You know, I've been thinking . . ." and ended three minutes later with me gently—but definitely—relieved from my new leadership position and moved back into the role of a frontline salesperson.

I had been, in fact, un-promoted. After three weeks.

I set my fork down, feeling sick to my stomach, and that was the end of my first leadership role *and* my love of powdered sugar.

Fortunately, my employer, FranklinCovey, one of the world's largest leadership-development organizations, offered me a second chance—many second chances. Through coaching and painful self-reflection, I learned to lead in a way that accomplished business results while developing my team.

After four years as a successful individual producer, I was re-extended the opportunity to lead, this time for a group of fifteen experienced salespeople in our higher-education division. By this time, I knew how to hold accountability meetings, review pipelines, forecast, understand what was a real sales opportunity and what wasn't. I was good at managing sales . . . which is very different from managing people.

That crucial transition didn't happen until I was promoted to general manager of our Midwestern region. It required a whole different level of skill, a more sophisticated strategy, more compassion, and tough calls. I had to interview and hire dozens of people . . . and also fire a few when their contributions fell short. I had to learn to develop high performers, motivate low performers, and have difficult conversations. I had to make decisions with six-figure consequences weekly.

It was through this role that I learned to become the manager my team deserved. To guide forty people with lofty career dreams, 401(k)s, mortgages, and families who depended on them, I had to bring a completely new level of maturity, wisdom, and judgment. I also had to earn my leadership position—it didn't automatically come with the title. I had to behave my way to credibility.

Around this time, my mentor told me, "Scott, ten years from now, no one will remember if you met your second-quarter EBITDA or increased your margin by 4 percent. Of course, you must deliver business results to earn the right to have and keep your leadership role, but your legacy will be the lives you influence and the careers you grow." I'd seen my mentor achieve stellar business results, but more importantly, I saw him model, coach, and instill confidence in others, changing lives for the better in the process. I began trying to do the same.

From living through this transition personally—and painfully—I became determined to help others through it. My coauthors, Todd and Victoria, share this passion and bring their own leadership challenges and experiences to this book. Ultimately, we realized that a guide with real people's experiences, combined with FranklinCovey's research, could help a lot of managers.

We've collected everything we've learned here to teach you, support you, and help you lead with confidence: insights into how and why great leaders think the way they do; nuts-and-bolts best practices for confronting and overcoming your most common leadership difficulties; tools and resources, including checklists, stories, and examples. *Everyone Deserves a Great Manager* delivers the guidance you hoped for when you were promoted but perhaps didn't receive: the support, understanding, strategies, and tactics to develop as a leader and turn your people into an engaged, high-performing team.

YOUR ROLE MATTERS MORE THAN EVER

These pages will benefit leaders at all levels, but first-level leaders (people who lead teams of individual contributors who themselves have no direct reports) will find this book especially valuable.

First-level leaders have never been more relevant. Executive adviser and bestselling author Ram Charan observes that the rapid digitization of information has eliminated massive layers of leadership in organizations. Work is collapsing down, not up. Which means that the vast majority of people are reporting to first-level leaders, who now assume unprecedented influence and responsibility.

For example, *Harvard Business Review* writes, "About 20% of the world's websites are now on the WordPress platform—making it one of the most important internet companies. And yet, Automattic, the firm behind WordPress, only employs a couple hundred people, who all work remotely, with a highly autonomous flat management structure."* Decades ago, the company would have had an organizational chart like a London Underground map; now a few developers on a Slack channel keep one-fifth of the web going.

In the "olden" days, first-level leaders had multiple managers above them who had steadily climbed the leadership ladder, accumulating experience along the way. Junior managers could draw on their expertise for mentorship and feedback. But today, most of those layers are gone, often leaving first-level leaders without sufficient resources or support.

In this role, you're supposed to know the strengths and weaknesses of your team members, appear to have all the answers, and transition from focusing on your own results to achieving the team's results. Overnight. You have to make sound decisions under ambiguous conditions, hold people accountable, and hit goals you may have had nothing to do with setting.

Despite being the new performance linchpin in your organization, you're often the least experienced and least trained. You're learning by trial and error because you have no other choice. Researchers in the *Harvard Business Review* found that, on average, people take on their first leadership role at age thirty—but don't receive their first leadership *training* until they're forty-two. As the researchers said, "They're operating within the company untrained, on average, for over a decade."† Imagine a physician, a pilot, or an engineer operating untrained for a decade—it's unfathomable. Why would we tolerate a lower standard for the linchpins of our organizations?

---

* Kastelle, T. (2019, March 01). "Hierarchy Is Overrated." Retrieved from https://hbr .org/2013/11/hierarchy-is-overrated.

† Zenger, J. (2014, August 07). "We Wait Too Long to Train Our Leaders." Retrieved from https://hbr.org/2012/12/why-do-we-wait-so-long-to-trai.

> ### Leadership vs. Management
>
> You may have noticed already that we use the terms "leader" and "manager" fairly interchangeably throughout this book. We did this consciously and aren't trying to further reinforce the divide between the two by elevating one over the other. What we do know is that some leaders need to be better managers, and some managers need to be better leaders. We'll leave philosophical definitions to some academic tome, so don't get hung up when we use one term or the other.

FranklinCovey has spent nearly four decades researching leadership, and we've found that first-level leaders are increasingly frustrated by the lack of mentoring, overburdened by impossible demands on their time, and worried about conducting difficult conversations. And if they don't have a path forward, the odds are high that they're going to abandon leadership—and maybe their employer too.

We know your role is difficult, but it is worth doing—and doing well—because you can truly improve the lives and careers of your team members. That's not hyperbole. Work stress can manifest as physical, mental, and emotional challenges for everyone, including you. As a leader, you will have an impact (for better or worse) on your team's ability to successfully overcome those challenges. We are committed to helping you become the manager both you and your team deserve.

THE 6 CRITICAL PRACTICES FOR LEADING A TEAM

To give you the confidence and competence you need to meet the inevitable challenges of managing, FranklinCovey has shrunk the bewildering world of first-level leadership down to the six most critical practices for leading a team:

Practice 1: Develop a Leader's Mindset

Practice 2: Hold Regular 1-on-1s

Practice 3: Set Up Your Team to Get Results

Practice 4: Create a Culture of Feedback

Practice 5: Lead Your Team Through Change

Practice 6: Manage Your Time and Energy

These practices have been field-tested by thousands of actual leaders working with real teams. This content expands upon FranklinCovey's leadership solution *The 6 Critical Practices for Leading a Team*, now adopted by thousands of companies, governments, nonprofits, school systems, and universities around the world.

Here's why you'll find this book valuable:

- **You'll learn how to make the biggest career transition of your life.** These practices will help you make the mental leap to leadership, without sacrificing the qualities that made you a high-performing individual contributor (often these two are at odds!).

- **You can apply the practices immediately.** Whether you're trying to lead a team of six or sixty, you need tools you can put to work today. Each practice is packed with step-by-step instructions you can put into action right now.

- **You'll get up to speed quickly.** We've distilled decades of research, hundreds of leader interviews, and tens of thousands of assessments down to the practices that yield the greatest results for first-level leaders.

More Experienced Leaders Can Use the 6 Practices Too

While we wrote this book for first-level leaders, mid- and senior-level leaders will also find a great deal of value in it. These are skills every leader needs to draw on and frequently revisit. Even if you're managing five hundred people, you know not to get complacent about the fundamentals. For more seasoned managers, this book is part refresher, part midcourse correction, and a collection of enduring principles that you can use to coach the first-level leaders who report to you.

Read this book cover to cover and keep it on your desk when you need specific information or tools. The book's structure is made for immersive study or on-demand enlightenment.

Your coaches over the following pages will be Todd Davis, Victoria Roos Olsson, and me, Scott Miller. As FranklinCovey's chief people officer, Todd brings expertise in talent development, building winning cultures, and unleashing the potential of your most precious asset: how your people collaborate. Todd will serve as your mentor on developing effective work relationships, as he has for hundreds of others throughout his career and in his recent bestseller *Get Better: 15 Proven Practices to Build Effective Relationships at Work*.

Do I want to be a great leader . . . or do I want my team to be led by a great leader?

One question is about me, and one is about them.

If I want to be a great leader, I might unknowingly see leadership through my lens—what builds my brand, my credibility, my career. If I shift my focus to wanting my team to have a great leader, I don't care about getting the credit. I want my team to reach its full potential, whether anybody knows I did that or not.

When my father passed away, we discovered that, over his lifetime, he'd anonymously helped dozens of people. He served with the goal of lifting others, not seeking credit for himself. The best leaders do the same.

All of us want to be recognized, at least a little. But focusing on others can be the most rewarding part of our career.

—TODD

Victoria, a Swedish senior leadership consultant for FranklinCovey, brings an international perspective and a true practitioner's approach. You'll benefit from her two decades of experience developing leaders—and leading many teams herself—in large organizations around the world, from Beijing to Dubai to Brussels. As a certified yoga instructor, Victoria will also help you bring the "whole person" into your leadership approach.

I will always remember when my friend Sofia called me on a Sunday evening with exciting news: she'd been promoted into her very first leadership role. Elated and a little nervous, she asked me to share everything I knew about being a great leader . . . in a half hour.

She was starting her new assignment the following day because it had been a quick, internal promotion. I shared as much as I could that Sunday evening, but any new leader needs more than a few minutes to make the biggest leap of their career.

This situation is all too common. There are a lot of Sofias out there—first-level leaders both excited and overwhelmed by their new responsibilities, thrown into their new role with just a "congratulations." This book is for all of you.

—VICTORIA

And I bring two decades of leadership mistakes, lessons learned, and successes, from my first un-promotion to finding my footing as a sales leader, general manager, executive vice president, and chief marketing officer. Like my two coauthors, I've intentionally chosen to be both candid and vulnerable so you can benefit from our collective leadership experiences. Hopefully, our transparency will give you a path around these common pitfalls. We pair these personal insights with learnings beyond FranklinCovey, including other respected leadership experts.

For clarity, I'll serve as your primary narrator, with the exception of Practice 6, where Victoria will bring her deep expertise. Please note that to honor confidences, we have changed some names and minor details in our stories.

Employees often report that their relationship with their direct leader is the most meaningful relationship in their professional lives, and determines whether they stay with a company or move on. If you become a great leader using the insights and skills in this book, you'll find greater job satisfaction, opportunities for advancement, and the chance to affect the lives of others for the better. You'll become the manager you and your team deserve.

Access More Tools Online

Visit everyonedeservesagreatmanager.com for more coaching from the authors. Check in as you read this book and whenever you need a refresher.

DEVELOP A LEADER'S MINDSET

I was raised in a stable middle-class family in central Florida. My brother and I rode our bikes to school, went to church on Sundays, and were tucked in bed by 7:30 p.m. sharp. We led a routine, predictable life, and I grew up thinking everyone lived this way. I was also taught to believe some specific things about life, most memorably that certain people always tell the truth and are always right: parents, police, and priests.

Uh-oh.

Do parents always tell the truth? Nope. Do police officers? Unfortunately, that isn't the case. Are all priests trustworthy? Horrifyingly not.

This was a limited *paradigm*, or mindset. Paradigms are the lenses through which we view the world, based on how we were raised, indoctrinated, and trained to see everything in front of us. We all wear these metaphorical pairs of glasses, and they vary in accuracy. They might be the right prescription or slightly off. In some cases, you might have a metaphorical cataract.

Mostly our mindsets are unconscious or subconscious. None of us (hopefully) set out in the morning to have biases or prejudices, but every one of us has them deeply ingrained in us from our experiences while we were raised. We often aren't even aware of them or their ongoing impact—negative and positive.

With the "parents, police, and priests" paradigm, I fortunately didn't have to put it to the test. I was generally surrounded by good examples of all three, but if I hadn't been so lucky, this paradigm could have caused serious damage. As it was, I didn't realize that parents were actually real people with flaws and weaknesses until my mid-twenties.

And it wasn't until I was in my thirties that I understood that *leaders* are people too—that they don't make all the right decisions or have all the right answers.

Your job as a leader is to continually assess your paradigms for accuracy and ensure they reflect reality. So ask yourself what you believe about leadership, your team, and yourself. Maybe you believe that the colleagues who think like you are "high potentials" and those who challenge you aren't. Perhaps you believe you're not *really* leadership material and someday everyone will find out.

TRY IT OUT ○

Assess Your Paradigms

List the members of your team. Write down your beliefs about each of them. Step back and ask, "What has happened that's made me think she's always late, he's sloppy, he's a know-it-all, or she's a genius?"

Are you giving them a fair shake? How much of your own fear, insecurity, jealousies, last interaction, or series of very valid encounters makes your assessment of them true or incomplete?

Now do the same for your paradigms about yourself. Do you have any strongly held beliefs that, if challenged or corrected, could increase your potential? Ask yourself, "Is this belief true? If not, how can I change it?"

Name: _____ Beliefs: _____

_____

Name: _____ Beliefs: _____

_____

Name: _____ Beliefs: _____

_____

—TODD

THE SEE-DO-GET CYCLE

I once went skiing with a good friend at Snowbird, a popular resort in Utah. Although she'd never skied down anything steeper than a bunny slope, I somehow convinced her that she could handle the Black Diamond run. "Come on, come on, come on!" I urged her. "No problem. Black Diamond! Woo-hoo!" And after luring her to the top, I gave her an encouraging shove.

She was taken down on a stretcher.

Horrified, I recently realized that I do this in my leadership role too. (And don't worry, my friend wasn't seriously injured and bounced back, no worse for the wear, although she's never skied again, at least with me.) While many leaders lack confidence in their people and tamp them down, I'm the opposite: I believe anyone can do anything if I just provide enough encouragement. I paint the vision and create excitement—whatever it takes to inspire them to my degree of confidence in them. My intention is to help people achieve their full potential . . . and who cares if they agree?

This paradigm sometimes works. But sometimes I accidentally lure people into terrible Black Diamond experiences instead. "No, you actually *can* do this. It's easy. It's only a speech to two thousand people. You'll do just fine."

When I'm putting people into jobs, assigning them to new territories or countries, putting them on stages in front of two thousand people, and contracting high-paying consulting gigs for them, the stakes are high. At worst, this paradigm can destroy people's confidences, reputations, and even careers, if we're not aligned.

I often need to rethink my approach and remember something we teach at FranklinCovey: the See-Do-Get Cycle. It's the root of real behavior change. When you challenge your mindset (tough work, by the way) you can make lasting changes to your actions and your results.

The See-Do-Get Cycle

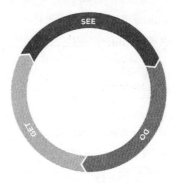

To best understand this cycle, let's start with our desired result, the "Get" part of the cycle. We all have different outcomes we're trying to achieve: improved health, meaningful relationships, financial stability, influence in our communities and careers—as well as short-term results we want from our day, meeting, or project.

What drives those results (Get) are our *behaviors*, the "Do" in this cycle. It's how we act. If we want to complete a report by the deadline, then we have to behave in a certain way throughout the day: check with the finance department about last quarter's profit and loss statement, resist distractions, etc. If we want to build rapport with our co-workers, we can invite them out to lunch. If we want to nail our presentation, we practice it over and over. You get the point.

Most people see that behavior and results are interconnected: what we *do* drives what we *get*. That is not an epiphany.

Here's what I think most people don't appreciate: the first crucial step, "See." This means that beyond our behavior, our results are affected by our mindset.

How we see things affects our behavior, which in turn affects our results.

Paradigm. Behavior. Result.

See. Do. Get.

If you want to get short-term results, change your behavior. You'll stop smoking—until a tense day at work. You'll wake up at 5 a.m. through sheer willpower—once, then hit snooze the rest of the week. You'll stop swearing—until you get cut off in traffic. Behavior changes will only net you a temporary fix.

As Dr. Stephen R. Covey taught, if you want to fundamentally change your results, if you want long-term sustainable impact, you have to challenge your mindset.

Having identified my "Black Diamond" paradigm, I wasn't happy with it. Sometimes it works, but not often enough—and my friend hanging up her skis made me rethink it. I reevaluated my paradigm about setting people up for success (See). Instead of relying on woo-hoos and enthusiasm, I help my team members develop their skills . . . after giving them a chance to opt out of my grand plans (Do). As a result, I've learned to grow people who are actually willing and ready (Get), and fortunately decreased the number of people I push down ski slopes.

Imagine a leader who has been assigned an important project to manage. If she closes this project successfully, it will be a great milestone in her career and might even lead to a coveted promotion.

But when she gets the list of people assigned to work on the project, the first thing that goes through her mind is, "Oh no, not those ten . . . they never put in any work and don't get anything right."

With this paradigm, will this leader sit down and listen to her team? Will she consider their input and viewpoints? Will she delegate important tasks? Doubtful. And when she does delegate simple, fail-proof things, she will probably double-check their work many times, also known as micromanaging.

Now imagine you are one of the people assigned to this team. The leader isn't listening to you or considering your ideas. She corrects everything you do. How would it make you feel? Would you prioritize this unpleasant project over your many other responsibilities? Would you bring your best talents, energy, and efforts to this project? Probably not.

Eventually, this leader will prove herself right. The way she saw the team members (paradigm) affected their behavior, which generated the result that nobody put in extra effort. Her initial impression was confirmed. She was right. Or was she?

—VICTORIA

FROM INDIVIDUAL CONTRIBUTOR TO LEADER

In tennis, what wins on grass and clay doesn't always translate to asphalt. When you win Wimbledon, you don't expect your coach's first conversation to be, "Congratulations, you won on grass! But now it's going to take a whole different approach to win on asphalt." You expect to be showered with accolades; instead you get an ego enema. The world of professional tennis is fraught with experts who were unable to transfer their superior play from one surface to another.

Likewise, I don't imagine that most high-performing, driven people promoted into leadership realize that they must now fundamentally change their approach. But many of the paradigms that got you promoted won't make you successful as a leader. You may be aware of Gallup's bestselling book *Now, Discover Your Strengths*. A subsequent book, *Dis-*

cover Your Sales Strengths, highlighted the conundrum high-producing salespeople face when they are "rewarded" with a promotion to become a sales leader. The strengths they perfected as an individual salesperson often included a strong sense of competition, a need for individual recognition and fame, and sometimes a zero-sum-game mentality—*I win; they lose*. Great for winning on the sales scoreboard, not so great for nurturing, coaching, and leading your team (as in, those people who might have been your peers yesterday).

TRY IT OUT ✪

Assess Your Leadership Paradigms

Identify the paradigms that made you successful as an individual contributor. For example:

- My own work is my number-one priority.
- I should always be prepared with the right answer.
- My validation comes from recognition of my performance.

Determine which of them will and won't work in your leadership role.

Talk to other successful leaders about the mindsets they had to leave behind when they transitioned from individual contributor to leader. What new beliefs did they adopt that have helped them?

—TODD

Across most professions, this perilous chasm exists: teacher to principal, server to restaurant manager, physician to chief of medicine. Or as the bestselling book by Marshall Goldsmith states, *What Got You Here Won't Get You There*. Fundamentally, becoming a leader will require you to let go of some of the skills and mindsets that made you successful as an individual contributor.

In the best of worlds, your manager would sit you down, talk about your strengths and why you were promoted, then explain what you're going to need to do differently going forward. If you don't receive that feedback, you have this book. We'll introduce each of the practices with a key mindset shift leaders *must* make to accomplish results. Circle which one tends to describe you at this point in time. (Don't know? Ask your team—they'll definitely have an opinion.)

PRACTICE	COMMON MINDSET	EFFECTIVE MINDSET
1. Develop a Leader's Mindset	I achieve results on my own.	I achieve results with and through others.
2. Hold Regular 1-on-1s	I hold 1-on-1s to monitor people's progress.	I hold regular 1-on-1s to help people get—and stay—engaged.
3. Set Up Your Team to Get Results	I tell team members what to do and how to do it.	I help team members get clear about the "why" behind the "what" and support them in the "how."
4. Create a Culture of Feedback	I give feedback so I can fix people's problems.	I give *and* seek feedback to elevate the entire team.
5. Lead Your Team Through Change	I control and contain change for my team.	I champion change with my team.
6. Manage Your Time and Energy	I am too busy to take time for myself.	I must manage my time and energy to be an effective leader.

PRACTICE 1 MINDSET SHIFT

I once worked with a record-setting salesperson, Carolyn. When a sales-manager position opened up, it was a no-brainer to promote her. Everybody assumed she would seamlessly transition from hitting—and often exceeding—her number quarter after quarter to helping her new team do the same.

That didn't happen. Instead, if her salespeople faltered during a client meeting, Carolyn would swoop in and use her extraordinary sales skills to close the deal. She thought she was saving the day. She was, but *only* that day. Her team didn't develop their own selling skills because Carolyn wouldn't let them make mistakes and recover from them. This is a common new-manager mistake: relying on your individual contributor skills—and doing everything yourself as soon as there is a problem—rather than helping your team solve the problem and learn. In the process, you lose your new team's trust. Carolyn was so focused on helping get the sale, what she knew she was good at and could do, that she lost sight of a critical reality: her new role was no longer about her hitting the number—it was to have *her team* hit the number.

COMMON MINDSET	EFFECTIVE MINDSET
I achieve results on my own.	I achieve results with and through others.

TRY IT OUT ⟳

Hold a Funeral for Your Old Job

If you derive a lot of satisfaction and validation from your previous accomplishments (and there's no shame in that!), you might need to say goodbye to them. Box up your trophies, awards, and certificates. If you're feeling really ambitious, take them to a safe spot and light them on fire— a sort of Burning Man(ager).

—VICTORIA

When you become a leader, your definition of results needs to change. You need to see them differently. When you were an individual contributor, your results were the work you did. But now you're a first-level leader, so you own the results of *everybody* on your team. Your first job is not to get results alone, but with and through others. You're still responsible for your personal deliverables, but they take a back seat to ensuring that your direct reports hit theirs, while the people on your team grow, learn, and even become leaders themselves. In other words: *your people* are your results.

You might be thinking, "I didn't even hire these people!" But part of your job is to discern the talent, coachability, and potential of each member of your team, whether you hired or inherited them. You have to learn who can—or can't—rise to the new standard you're requiring. But before you consider dismissing an employee, remember that they might just need a leader who can challenge and inspire them to a new level of contribution. That leader might be you.

What if Carolyn didn't save the day during sales meetings? Yes, her team would make mistakes. Some deals might not close. But her team would learn from those errors, especially if she followed up with feedback and coaching, and they would probably get better results in the future. Just as important, she would show that she trusted her team, rather than treat them like rookies who needed hand-holding. The result would be savvier, more skilled, and confident salespeople who collectively met their numbers (and weren't reliant on one person to save the day every time).

We recognize that some industries and settings have less or no tolerance for mistakes, due to safety, quality, and accuracy. In this case, leaders should work side by side with their team members for close accountability and modeling, without doing their job for them or suffocating them.

In my book *Get Better: 15 Proven Practices to Build Effective Relationships at Work*, I share an example of a leader who modeled the effective mindset of achieving results with and through others.

A hospitality executive oversaw a sprawling property with almost four thousand employees, which he said often felt more like running a city than a hotel. We'd partnered with them on leadership development, and he invited our executive team to meet his department heads to share their results: housekeeping, food and beverage, engineering, sales, catering, and more. Before they came in, he shared his vision for each of them, saying something like:

"I've worked here for more than twenty years and had a phenomenal run. I've been lucky to earn our President's Club Award many times. But now I have all the crystal trophies I could ever need. I want my team to earn President's Club and more, and then I want them to pass that same vision on to the people they lead. That's what I want my legacy to be."

And it wasn't just talk. When the department managers arrived, they clearly knew their leader wanted them to shine. It was one of the most productive and inspiring meetings I'd ever attended, and it changed my paradigm about how I lift my own team.

—TODD

If you have the common mindset of achieving results on your own, it's important to accept once and for all that your work isn't just about you anymore; it's about them. It's time to let go of your past successes. You earned the leader's chair because you performed at a superior level. Take a victory lap. Now, let it all go and focus on the job ahead.

BECOMING THE LEADER
YOUR TEAM DESERVES

Keep the following questions in mind while you read the rest of the practices. At the conclusion of this book, you'll take your insights and craft a plan for becoming the leader your team deserves.

- What kind of leader does your team need right now? What kind of leader does your organization need you to be?

- What do you need to learn (or unlearn) to become the leader they need?

- Picture yourself ten years from now. What do you want your team to say about this time in their lives? What results will you and your team have delivered? How would you want your team to describe your leadership?

- What do you need to do in the coming months to make your vision happen?

GETTING TO KNOW YOUR TEAM

In the wise words attributed to Abraham Lincoln, "I don't like that man. I must get to know him better." The only way to check your paradigms is to compare them to reality. One of the ways to assess and strengthen the collective capabilities of the team is to get to know them better.

Pick a few questions and go through this activity once a year as a team or whenever a new member joins the team. It's not a strategy to confirm your biases; it's an exercise to challenge your paradigms. Declare your intent beforehand, and encourage your team to share as much or as little as they're comfortable with.

Exercise Option A: Pair, share, and rotate. Everyone, including the manager, pair up and ask your partner one question from this list. After each person has answered at least one question, rotate to another partner and repeat. Continue rotating until each person talks to everyone else at least once. (If your team has an odd number, you may have a trio.)

Exercise Option B: Group share. As a group (or, if the team is too large, split into halves or thirds), go around in a circle and answer as many questions as appropriate. Determine beforehand whether the team wants to answer all or some of the questions, or limit the exercise by time.

1. What's something about your background that others at work may not know about you? For example: something about where you grew up, your family, culture, or beliefs.

2. What's important to you outside of work? For example: being physically active, community service, trying new restaurants, relaxing, or other hobbies.

3. Tell us about a prior job that had a big influence on who you are today. What did you like or not like about it?

4. Tell us about one of your goals. For example: a short-term goal related to your current role, a long-term career goal, or a personal goal.

5. What makes your job most rewarding? Tell us about what motivates you at work.

6. What's one thing you want people to know about how you like to communicate? For example: email vs. in person, or short bursts vs. long discussions.

7. What's one thing you want people to know about how you process feedback? For example: scheduled vs. in the moment, or active dialogue vs. sitting back and listening.

8. How do you like to be recognized? For example: in writing vs. in person, in public vs. in private? What do your preferences say about you?

9. Do you consider yourself introverted or extroverted? What situations draw out your introverted/extroverted side?

10. What types of personalities frustrate or fatigue you? How have you learned to collaborate more effectively with them?

Feel free to add your own questions that relate to your team's culture, challenges, or expertise. Did you learn anything surprising about your team members . . . or about yourself? Were any of your existing paradigms challenged? How will adjusting them affect your leadership?

Take a moment to review this practice, and note the insights that most resonated with you.

_____

_____

_____

_____

_____

_____

_____

_____

Jot down two to three action items you want to commit to.

_____

_____

_____

_____

_____

_____

_____

_____

HOLD REGULAR 1-ON-1s

Several years ago, we had a superstar project manager, Joanna, who worked remotely and led a team of junior project managers. Joanna was developing her team's capacities, hitting goals quarter after quarter, and doing extremely well financially—a low-maintenance high performer you could count on to deliver.

Then she handed in her two weeks' notice.

As chief people officer, I dropped everything to meet with her and convince her to stay. Did she get another offer somewhere else? better incentives? We'd match it!

But as we talked, Joanna made it clear those weren't the issues at all. Working from her home office made her feel disconnected from her team, and the way her manager spoke with her during their 1-on-1s only made things worse.

"He's a good guy," she told me. "But when we talk, it's just long enough for him to run through my projects. He acknowledges that they're always on time and on budget, but then the meeting is over. Never a question about the challenges of working remotely or what I'm interested in doing next. I know it's not his job to be my friend, but I want to work where I feel valued and connected—not just a machine."

I spoke with her manager about the issue but couldn't make much headway. He insisted that he'd love "time to chat" with each team member, but he had an overwhelming schedule.

As a last-ditch effort, I convinced Joanna to move to another team with a promising new leader. Because he was new to leadership, this leader was hyper-focused on the fundamentals. He met regularly with his team members individually. He asked them questions. He listened. He remembered that his employees were whole people with lives beyond work. He made an effort to draw in remote employees and encouraged the team to interact and collaborate.

Joanna flourished with this leader, not only tackling bigger goals than ever but also helping her peers do the same. I'm happy to report that she continues to be a superstar for our organization to this day.

We all work for more than a paycheck. We crave camaraderie, collaboration, and engagement, especially as fewer of us work in brick-and-mortar buildings.

What I especially appreciate about the experience with Joanna was that the newer leader understood this. It's not always about how many years you have under your belt as a leader. That can work against you if you unintentionally go on autopilot and forget that leaders need to address the emotional aspect of the job.

Now think about your leadership style—both who you are now and who you want to be. Analyze yourself: Are you more like Joanna's first leader, or her new one? Do you have any Joannas on your team? What could you do to find out? And how can you ensure that engaging your team members on a regular basis is job number one, no matter how busy you get?

—TODD

As we build the case that 1-on-1s are one of your strongest levers to engage your team, let's first define what we mean by "engagement." At FranklinCovey, we've found that employees typically fall on a spectrum, with a distinct difference between the bottom and top three levels:

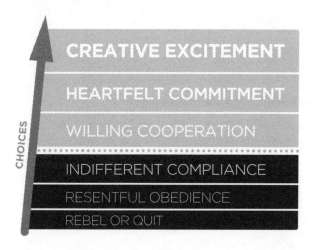

CHOICES

CREATIVE EXCITEMENT

HEARTFELT COMMITMENT

WILLING COOPERATION

INDIFFERENT COMPLIANCE

RESENTFUL OBEDIENCE

REBEL OR QUIT

Note the dotted line in the middle—it's key. Team members above the line are doing the job because they *want* to, while those below are doing the job because they *have* to. If people are indifferently compliant or lower, you will have to tell them over and over what to do, because they won't do it on their own.

While all leaders would love to have their teams at the top level, occasionally they say, "Some days, I'd take indifferent compliance!" It might be tempting just to get by, but don't settle—true engagement pays off. Gallup has consistently linked employee engagement with profitability, productivity, quality, and turnover.[*]

Leaders don't, in fact, create engagement. People *choose* their level of engagement. Leaders create the *conditions* for engagement—for better or worse.

As we saw with Joanna, a paycheck alone isn't enough to motivate your team to climb the levels. Neither are bonuses, offices, titles, praise, or even ultimatums and threats. Those may be easy to deploy, but their effectiveness fades fast. If we promise a direct report that they'll get a bonus if they land a critical project, their immediate performance may spike. But the next time we want to motivate them, we may have to pony up another bonus. That's not sustainable financially, but more importantly, it won't catalyze the engagement of your people long term.

---

[*] Gallup, Inc. (2013, June 20). How Employee Engagement Drives Growth. Retrieved from https://www.gallup.com/workplace/236927/employee-engagement-drives-growth.aspx.

TRY IT OUT ✪

Assess Your Team's Engagement

Place each of your team members on the level where you tend to see them most. Where would you put yourself? What's the average mark for your team? What would be different if the average moved up one level? Would you get any different results? You might not know where an individual falls and what it takes for them to move up the scale of engagement. If that's the case, effective 1-on-1s are going to be extra important.

And by the way, don't let this be a secret framework for your eyes only. Share and discuss it with your team (your overall team engagement, of course, not where you rank each individual). I love this model and often use it with my team members to identify where we are and what we can do to move up that scale of engagement.

—VICTORIA

In our experience, people rarely quit their jobs based on compensation; rather, they quit their manager. Or they quit the culture. So it's imperative to consider the conditions you are creating for a compelling work environment. Do you make it easy, engaging, and actually enjoyable to get work done, or are there too many processes making it difficult and unrewarding? Do you look over people's shoulders, closely monitoring their progress? Or maybe you abandon colleagues, leaving them to figure things out entirely on their own? Do you celebrate people, or do you let opportunities to acknowledge them pass you by? Do you give your team courageous yet considerate feedback? Do they feel safe telling you the truth? Is it too challenging or not challenging enough for team members to succeed in your culture—and do you notice when they do?

We often think of culture as a nebulous concept. But leaders create culture in every interaction, email, meeting, speech, or text. They also can destroy it in those interactions: talking about people behind their back, using an inappropriate tone in an email or a text, failing to give people credit, ignoring someone in the hallway, or complaining about company policies. Because you're a leader, you're noticed. Every time you communicate, every time you open your mouth, you create culture. And 1-on-1 interactions are one of your best tools to build and reinforce the type of culture every team member deserves. Strategically planned and executed, 1-on-1s are arguably the best way to create the conditions for high engagement and ensure your team members are connected to you as their leader.

COMMON MINDSET	EFFECTIVE MINDSET
I hold 1-on-1s to monitor people's progress.	I hold regular 1-on-1s to help people get—and stay—engaged.

Unfortunately, 1-on-1s often end up as status updates—if we hold them at all. They become rote meetings to check people's progress: "What did you work on last week? What are you working on this week? Great. Next!"

If our main interaction with our team members is to check that they've hit key benchmarks, we become our team's *monitor*. You might get incremental improvements this way, but you're just as likely to deflate people's energy, zap their creativity, and drive them to do the minimum.

By only monitoring progress, the leader in Todd's story missed the opportunity to discover that Joanna actually wanted connection more than another bonus. He thought he didn't have enough time to hold more in-depth 1-on-1s, so he saved thirty minutes a week in the short term, and lost one of his most high-performing employees in the long term.

In contrast, effective leaders use 1-on-1s to *coach*. They create the conditions for engagement by meeting regularly with each team member, drawing out issues through open-ended questions and Empathic Listening, and helping people solve problems.

In effective 1-on-1s, you might hear things like:

"A colleague is blocking my progress."

"My personal life is falling apart."

"I'm getting bored with my role."

"I have a great idea, but I haven't had time to think it through."

"I get really nervous when I give presentations, and I need help."

"I'm not sure what you expect."

Because information like this is uncovered, 1-on-1s have higher stakes than other kinds of meetings. And they take different skills. If we prepare beforehand and coach during these meetings, we can unearth challenges, head off problems, test new ideas, celebrate successes, and encourage growth.

SKILL 1: PREPARE FOR YOUR 1-ON-1s

First, let's establish some best practices for 1-on-1s. Schedule them in advance as recurring calendar appointments. Try to meet at the same day and time for each team member. Reserve at least thirty minutes, because it's difficult to have meaningful conversations in less time. Hold them regularly—the gold standard is weekly—and commit to that date and time without moving the appointment if possible.

HOW TO SAY IT

Announce 1-on-1s and Set Expectations with Your Team

Consider making a team announcement like this:

I'm going to start asking for 1-on-1 meetings with each of you. I want to be careful that they're valuable and that they follow a specific format: weekly or twice monthly, about thirty minutes long. They won't replace staff meetings. The purpose is for you to express concerns; let me know how you're feeling about your role, the organization, and your development; and call on me for help. Be realistic about what we can accomplish during the time. On average, I'm going to spend eighty percent of the time listening, coaching, and helping you solve problems.

I ask for your help scheduling and maintaining them. There will be some rocky paths when either party can't honor them. We need to pre-forgive each other. I'll do my best not to cancel, recognizing that sometimes I'll need to. Generally, we're heading in a new direction. What's important to remember is that these are your meetings, not mine. Be thoughtful about focusing on your highest-leverage items to grow your career, skills, and engagement, and help you feel like a winning member of this team.

—TODD

Don't cancel unless absolutely necessary. Canceling a 1-on-1 is a huge withdrawal—it clearly communicates to the team member that they're not important. It will be frighteningly easy to cancel the second, third, and fourth 1-on-1 after you've greased that track. Holding your second 1-on-1 is probably even more important than the first one. Same with the third. Once you're in, you have to stay in.

A good friend, Drew, told me about joining a new company. On his first day, his new boss shared with him what a great talent he was, what an important role he was filling, and how glad she was that he joined them. Drew's success was one of her top priorities, so she wanted to meet weekly to support him.

When their first meeting came around, Drew was buzzing with ideas and questions. But that morning, the boss's assistant apologetically called to reschedule. Something *important* had come up. Drew was disappointed, but said he understood and would look forward to their next meeting.

But the following week, Drew received another apologetic call from the assistant.

And no surprise—it happened the following week too. Before long, several months passed, and he still hadn't met with his manager outside of staff meetings.

Drew learned from his co-workers that this was a common pattern and that he shouldn't expect it to change. The excitement of his new role diminished, and his morale sank to the point that he thought about quitting. Instead, he resigned himself to just getting through his to-do list each day.

The canceled 1-on-1s sent a clear message: Drew wasn't a priority, and his engagement didn't matter.

—TODD

Often you'll be tempted to cancel your 1-on-1s when your own boss has demanded something urgent from you. Proactively assess when your boss is most likely to commandeer your time and see if you can schedule your 1-on-1s when they have a sacred meeting that they're unlikely to cancel. Depending on your culture and relationship with your leader, you might also consider framing it as a question for them: "I have a regularly scheduled 1-on-1 with Tina at that time. Do you want me to cancel on her?" With some thoughtfulness, you can think through the temptations and distractions likely to come your way.

Prepare an agenda. Collect your thoughts ahead of time and ask your team member to do the same. Avoid talking about the same things over and over.

HELPFUL TOOL ⬡

1-on-1 Meeting Planner

Sometimes leaders think they should know everything by heart, never missing a detail, and give that appearance to their team. I often advise leaders to use tools and resources to help them, and to not be afraid of showing their teams that they do. After all, that's how you create the culture of preparing and learning in order to achieve results. I usually write down the key questions I want to ask and the most important points I want to cover prior to the meeting. I never try to hide that; on the contrary, I often share it. It sets the tone that I want my team members to do the same.

We've included 1-on-1 prep worksheets for you and your team members at the end of this chapter. The worksheets have been field-tested by thousands of leaders. Use them as they are or customize them for your team.

—VICTORIA

Remember that the purpose of this meeting is to lift the engagement of your team member. Let them be part of creating the agenda or invite them to take the lead. The format may vary—sometimes one or both of you will fill out an agenda planner like the ones at the end of this chapter; sometimes you'll lead, sometimes they will. Whatever the structure, remember the point is to lift their engagement. One constant: you're not going to have more time than you need, so be realistic about priorities and put the most important items up front, including the issues that require the most conversation, assessment, or brainstorming.

Account for your energy. In his recent bestseller *When: The Scientific Secrets of Perfect Timing*, Daniel Pink discussed the concept of understanding your energy peaks, troughs, and recovery. Ask yourself at what point of the day are you at your highest levels of energy—physically and intellectually? At what points are you at your lowest? I've realized my peak is from 5 a.m. to 10 a.m. when I do my best creative thinking and collaborating. I execute on those ideas at a fevered pace until 11:30 a.m., when I become fixated on lunch. My trough hits in the afternoon.

Now that I know this, I need to schedule my 1-on-1s in the morning so my team gets my finest attention and discipline, and I'm least likely to cancel them. Don't schedule 1-on-1s when your energy wanes or schedule them back-to-back without a break. And, of course, you'll never find the perfectly optimal time, but consider your team member's energy level as well. Although we generally recommend keeping the appointment time consistent, you might want to rotate your meeting time if there's a conflict between your energy needs and theirs.

Adjust for remote 1-on-1s. If part or all of your team is remote from you, you'll need to modify your 1-on-1s. Without daily in-person interaction, it's easy to miss subtle cues about how they're doing. You'll likely need extra time to talk—and listen—about their concerns, questions, and progress.

CONSIDER THIS ⑦

1-on-1s Can Save Time in the Long Term

You might see adding weekly 1-on-1s with your team members to your calendar as a lot of extra work and time. But holding them regularly might actually save you time. This might be the perfect solution to avoid interruptions and last-minute urgent tasks that result from not having regular individual check-ins with your team.

—VICTORIA

I was recently consulting with an organization that had a team member working remotely on the other side of the country. She only saw her team in person three to four times a year. I asked her how she liked working out of her home after a career in an office, and she said, "I like the flexibility, but sometimes the silence is deafening."

- **Break up remote 1-on-1s over multiple days.** Try scheduling shorter, more frequent 1-on-1s so there's less time between meetings and an extra chance to pick up on brewing issues.
- **Respect time zones.** When scheduling, be considerate of what time it is on your team member's side of the world—and how that affects your team member's peak, trough, and recovery times.

- **Use face-to-face tools.** Leaders need to be aware of how lonely and disconnected virtual members might feel. It's hard to create culture sitting alone at the kitchen table. Whenever possible, conduct your virtual 1-on-1s on video so you can see their body language and facial expression. Don't underestimate the power of video conferencing with remote employees—it could be the difference between them staying engaged in the culture and abandoning it.

CONSIDER THIS ⑦

Use Video to Increase Engagement

I was recently working with a manager on a performance plan for a particular team member. One of the issues was the team member's level of engagement. The manager noted that during their weekly team calls with many remote members, this employee was the only one who didn't join those calls using video (she used only audio). While it may sound like a small thing, it truly lowered the level of engagement, and the manager was left to wonder how present this employee really was.

Video is more than just convenient. In this virtual age of working, it has become more and more the norm for how we connect with others, so don't take it lightly. Remember, if you don't use video, you cut out the huge percentage of communication that comes through body language and expression.

You want to set the culture by encouraging all remote team members to attend virtual meetings via video—and modeling it yourself.

—TODD

Now for some real talk. When done properly and methodically, 1-on-1s can change your culture of engagement. But they could also destroy it when done haphazardly or, worse, not honored at all.

Think carefully about how you're going to ease into this practice, because it differs drastically from holding performance appraisals once a year or quarter. When I was working with a client recently, I introduced the practice of holding regular 1-on-1s to the team leader, Chris. He immediately realized the opportunity to grow the business and help his team of thirty connect to him as the leader, and got excited to announce it to his team the next day. But I cautioned him, "Chris, be careful about announcing that you're now going to hold 1-on-1s every week with every member of the team. Because if you're like most leaders, you're going to overcommit yourself, burn out, and start canceling. And it will actually decrease the level of trust you have with your team."

You don't want to fall into the trap of announcing 1-on-1s with everyone when you might not be able to keep that promise. Once you open your calendar, reality will set in. With simple thoughtfulness, Chris recalibrated: "Okay, what can I actually accomplish? Could it be monthly?" Once a month was 100 percent more than what he was currently doing. As much as he recognized the value of instituting regular 1-on-1s, he also recognized the importance of not overcommitting.

Holding regular 1-on-1s requires a level of discipline and perseverance that will be constantly tested by urgent requests, distractions, and needs coming down from your own leader. It challenges the conventional paradigm that bosses run meetings and address their own priorities. It's possible that you've been craving this meeting with your own leader, but they haven't made the time for it. You need to summon the maturity, stamina, and vision to decide you're going to be the leader your people need, not based on the leader you may have.

Don't underestimate how difficult but impactful and rewarding these meetings can be. You're going to need to continually revise your thinking about what happens during this meeting, your role vs. their role, how much time you listen vs. speak, and perhaps most importantly, the damage that comes from not honoring them. You may not be recognized for keeping them, but you will be made a pariah for canceling them.

Be measured. Calibrate. Be realistic. Don't overcommit. Although we recommend holding them weekly, your cadence will be based on

EVERYONE DESERVES A GREAT MANAGER

your day job, your number of direct reports, your other commitments, and the demands of your own boss. If your team is large, you might decide to hold them every two or four weeks so you don't implode under the weight of your commitment.

SKILL 2: COACH DURING THE 1-ON-1

In this practice, we're shifting from monitors of actions to coaches of people. That requires you to no longer tell people what to do, but to ask them how they would do it; from having all the answers to helping people discover the answers; from checking boxes to asking meaningful questions—and really listening to their answers. When you make this transition, you'll move from directing and informing to inspiring and engaging.

Coaching means respecting your team members' abilities and believing they have the capacity to grow. It means encouraging them to problem-solve, think in new ways, and develop their talents. Some colleagues will resist solving their own problems because they lack confidence. Coaching builds that confidence and minimizes dependencies.

CONSIDER THIS ⑦

Meet Them Where They Are

I conduct a lot of 1-on-1s in my role, many of them quite sensitive. Before every meeting, I remind myself to try to get in the other person's shoes. I think over the topics we will be discussing and try to "meet them where they are." I use this phrase to remember I really want to connect with them. That doesn't mean I plan to agree with them on every topic; it means I try to see things from their perspective, to get in their frame of reference. "I wonder how Greg is coping with his recent promotion. I know he thinks he has too many graphic designers reporting to him, and he's missing deadlines. Is he feeling overwhelmed?"

Thinking through the meeting beforehand helps me have empathy and identify ways to help the person with whom I'm meeting. Some leaders say this feels too mechanical. If it's not something you've done before, it may feel awkward at first. But if your intent is to develop your team, it will become natural in short order, enabling you to positively influence those you are leading.

—TODD

To coach well, you must be fully present. Whether you're conducting the meeting live or virtually, remove as many distractions as possible. Close your laptop and put any tasks away from your line of sight. Resist looking at your phone every time it vibrates.

Giving someone your undivided attention—truly rare these days—can signal profound respect for the team member. When the meeting starts, I recommend intentionally placing your phone on silent and putting it away, in order to demonstrate that they have your full attention. Literally do this in front of the other person. It may seem a bit contrived, but it's a tangible sign that they are your top priority for the next thirty minutes.

During a particularly stressful time at work and home, I still took pride in keeping my commitment of holding my 1-on-1s with my team members. But to be honest, while I was physically there, I wasn't mentally present. I was "ticking the box." I thought I hid it well.

But when I asked my team members for feedback on the previous quarter's 1-on-1 meetings, two of them told me that I seemed preoccupied and that my mind was elsewhere.

I was embarrassed that my lack of attention had been so transparent! But that wasn't the real issue. I didn't need to learn better techniques to hide my preoccupation; I needed a strategy to stay focused and give my team members the attention they deserved.

Since receiving that feedback, I take ten minutes before each 1-on-1 to review the previous meeting's notes, turn off my email notifications, and silence my phone. After a few deep breaths and quiet time to reflect and focus, I feel much more present during the meetings. And my team members notice too.

Get feedback on whether the 1-on-1s are adding value, and discuss what you both can do to improve the meetings.

—VICTORIA

Try to take care of anything urgent that could arise during the meeting beforehand, and let those around you know not to interrupt. An employee might become emotional during a 1-on-1, and the last thing you want is for them to feel like someone will walk in during a vulnerable moment. If you meet in an open-concept space or an office with glass walls, establish appropriate privacy before the meeting. Perhaps keep tissues discreetly nearby. A little thoughtfulness goes a long way. People will remember how you handle these moments.

Ask Coaching Questions

Coaching questions are open-ended and can't be answered with a simple yes or no. They encourage reflection and invite team members to do the majority of the talking and solve their own problems.

Instead of: "Are you liking your job?"	Ask: "What do you like about your role? What would you like to see change?"
Instead of: "Everything going okay?"	Ask: "What's the biggest challenge you're facing right now?"
Instead of: "Here's what I'd do . . ." or "Have you considered . . ."	Ask: "How did you approach this situation last time? Why do you think that worked (or not)?"

At the end of this chapter, we've gathered an extensive list of coaching questions to address challenging situations (e.g., helping a team member solve a problem on their own, getting your 1-on-1s out of a rut, and drawing out a difficult issue). Before your 1-on-1s, add the most relevant questions to your prep worksheet or agenda. Any one of those questions could take up your whole 1-on-1—and that's perfectly fine. Go with the flow and get the conversation going.

CONSIDER THIS ?

Coaching Former Peers and Other Smart People

You might find yourself managing people who used to be your peers, which can be uncomfortable at first. With them or very senior members on my team, I've made the mistake of expecting that they don't need me, even thinking that if I asked if they needed my help or if I gave advice, it would feel condescending.

On one particular occasion, I truly failed. The new recruit was so senior that I expected her to make it on her own, without any support or coaching from me. But this turned out to be lose-lose. Because my expectations were so high, she was hesitant to ask for help and I didn't realize until it was too late that she was struggling.

If you only communicate "I expect great things from you," people believe that you expect them to do everything on their own. I should have sat down with this senior employee and clarified together what she was comfortable handling on her own and where she needed my support.

Since then, when I hire other very experienced people, I take time to diagnose their knowledge and confidence. I don't assume anything from their résumé. I spend more time trying to understand how much coaching they need. I'm also careful to establish that I'm there to support and coach them, and they should use me as their sounding board.

If you just ask your team members if they need support, a lot of people will say no—unless you've established that supporting your team is exactly why you're there.

—VICTORIA

For your first 1-on-1, you won't naturally switch from a traditional meeting approach, where you're monitoring results and providing solutions, to a coaching model, without some practice. Try role-playing it with a trusted peer to practice moving from talking 80 percent of the time to 20 percent, from leading the meeting to following, from solving to coaching.

LISTEN WITH EMPATHY

During a 1-on-1 with Allison, whom I've worked with for more than a decade, she began to share a challenge I happened to be fairly passionate about. I immediately flipped into problem-solving mode, spouting ideas, grilling her with questions, and then interrupting her to answer them myself. Finally Allison said in exasperation, "*If you would just shut up, I'd tell you.*"

It stopped me in my tracks. What was I doing? I had violated every part of the 1-on-1 and caused one of my most effective (and polite) team members to blow a gasket. And she was totally in the right.

Listening is a vastly undervalued leadership competency. We're taught the importance of clarifying our messages, communicating with confidence and persuasion, and mastering the specific words we use. At most, we give some lip service to the value of just shutting up and listening. It's counterintuitive as a leader, because we've often spent our careers talking—setting a vision others want to follow; convincing; instructing. Those are hard to do silently.

Listening is hard work. It requires you to suspend your own needs and check into someone else's. It necessitates self-control, discipline, and a genuine interest in understanding another's point of view. Listening requires you to care.

Too often in our current world of showmanship, listening can be viewed as weakness. Telling—now that's a strength. TED Talks, for example, are built on telling . . . faster.

Here's a listening technique that's helped me over the years, modified from an original version by Deborah Tannen, the famed Georgetown University professor of linguistics and communication expert. When someone else is talking, purposely close your mouth and ensure your lips touch each other (your own lips, not yours to theirs). If your upper and lower lips are touching, it's impossible to speak. Try it. You literally can't form a word, thus you can't interrupt. Don't overexaggerate it. Just close your mouth, gently keep your lips touching, and listen.

There's more. When the other person is finished talking, keep your lips together, count to three, or even five. If you remain silent, the likelihood that they will keep talking is high. It's during this second "round" of listening that the other person may share vital, relevant, even touching details about their point of view.

I'm convinced that the first step to becoming a better listener is to simply stop talking and eliminate, or even just lessen, your own interrupting.

Once while leading a diverse team of individuals from several different countries, I knew my ability to truly understand would be critical to our success. I was consciously using silence during 1-on-1s to get to the heart of different issues.

I even overheard one team member say to another, "You always end up talking more than you expect when you walk into her office." My goal wasn't to uncover people's secrets, but to understand their viewpoints. What motivated them? Why did they act in a certain way? What experiences had given them their unique perspectives?

Being comfortable with silence gave my team members the space they needed to ponder, explore, and share. And it gave me time to listen deeply and allow important issues to surface naturally, which helped me see the bigger picture and become a better coach and leader.

I have learned to use silence to communicate better. It took a while since I'm normally a chatty person. But when I was given the nickname "Queen of Silence" by my team, I had proof that listening is a leadership skill you can learn and develop.

—VICTORIA

Contrast interrupting with Empathic Listening, or listening with the intent to understand. The essence of Empathic Listening is not that you agree or disagree with someone; it's that you fully, deeply understand that person, emotionally as well as intellectually. Suspend your thinking long enough to get inside another person's frame of reference, looking out through it, and trying to sincerely see the world the way they see it. You understand their paradigm and begin to understand how they feel.

Empathy is not sympathy. Sympathy is a form of agreement and sometimes is appropriate for the situation. But some people feed on sympathy, and it makes them further dependent . . . on you.

Empathic Listening requires you to pay attention to what they're saying, and their body language as well. You listen for feeling, meaning, and behavior. Then check for understanding:

"So what you're saying is . . ."

"Let me make sure I'm hearing you correctly . . ."

"It seems as if you're upset about this. Is that right . . . ?"

Be careful not to overuse these phrases. Make sure you deploy them sincerely, or they may come off too studied or as a technique. The key is to try to understand the other person's point of view. Great leaders continue to do this *after* the conversation, by synthesizing common themes they hear during the 1-on-1, setting goals based on these conversations, and implementing changes accordingly. You're going to have much better results with your 1-on-1s if you approach them as a continuous conversation and not just a thirty-minute hoop to jump through.

––––––––––

Recently a team member came to me for advice about a serious issue. I listened and helped her find a solution. It was a good one-hour proper coaching chat. She left happy.

The next day someone from the same department wanted to talk to me. I didn't have time, but he started off in a very similar way as the person the day before. I thought, "Hey, I can help him because I already solved this problem yesterday!" A couple of sentences from him triggered my entire response. I gave him the same advice and rushed off to my meeting.

Only because I had a good relationship with him did I find out that my advice led to complete disaster. I had to apologize, go back, and truly listen. And, of course, I learned that his issue was a different one and required different advice. Instead of having to undo the damage I had accidentally created by trying to rush through his problem, I should have set up a separate time to listen to him.

Many managers say they're bad at listening when they're stressed or have negative feelings. I actually don't listen well when I'm super enthusiastic. I go right into solving problems—even if it's not the actual problem that needs solving.

When do you tend to slip out of listening mode?

—VICTORIA

Dr. Stephen R. Covey said, "The deepest need of the human heart is to feel understood." Slow down the next time you're in a conversation where emotions are high. Listen for what the other person is *really* saying. Stretch yourself to look through another person's frame of reference.

CREATE COMMITMENTS AT THE END OF THE 1-ON-1

A pushback I often get with Empathic Listening is "I don't want to become the office therapist" or "When does Empathetic Listening end? When do we finally get to problem solving?"

While listening is clearly essential (and the part most leaders struggle with), 1-on-1s also require you to share insights, ideas, and frameworks to coach, support, and develop your team members.

For example, one of my team members was starting to feel discouraged about not reaching his targets. By carefully listening during our 1-on-1s, I detected his frustration and we discussed how it was impacting his engagement. But I didn't leave it there. We then devised a plan to improve his sales calls and reach his goals. It wasn't enough to listen; he needed hands-on coaching and advice.

Coaching is more than asking questions and listening; it's keeping each other accountable for what you've discussed and taking action. If you're focused on engagement throughout your 1-on-1, your team member should feel ownership over their responsibilities, and excitement at the prospect of accomplishing their goals.

Wrap up by reviewing any action items from last week. If they didn't complete the previous week's commitments, you should listen, understand the reason, and coach your team member about how to move forward. Address the issue early before it becomes a trend. Then agree on next steps. Don't fall into the trap of telling your team member what to do; let them articulate their commitments. You'll learn in Practice 3 how to delegate effectively and give feedback if things aren't going well—for example, if a team member is constantly missing deadlines.

One way you can help your team is by clearing the path—cutting through bureaucratic red tape, connecting the team member with a contact, or getting a response from someone who's been unavailable. This is especially helpful for someone you're managing whose job is outside of your technical expertise. Ask, "What can I do this week to support you?" or "What resources can I provide?" Then get it done. Keeping your commitments is just as important as employees keeping theirs.

1-ON-1 PLANNERS

Use the worksheets below to plan your 1-on-1s or modify them as needed. They'll help you ask relevant questions in your next 1-on-1 and make the time more valuable for both of you.

In addition to helping you prepare for your 1-on-1s, these worksheets will help you keep a record of your conversations. Many managers are so busy or have so many direct reports, that they forget what they spoke about in their last 1-on-1. If you don't remember what you talked about last week, you've lost time and momentum.

Note: You'll learn more about reinforcing and redirecting feedback in Practice 4.

1-ON-1 PLANNER FOR MANAGERS

DATE:	TEAM MEMBER:

CHECK-IN, DEVELOPMENT GOALS, AND FEEDBACK

Outcome and follow-up items from previous 1-on-1:	
The person's overall development goals:	
Current development focus:	
Reinforcing feedback I want to give:	
Redirecting feedback I want to give:	

EVERYONE DESERVES A GREAT MANAGER

1-ON-1 PLANNER FOR MANAGERS

DATE:	TEAM MEMBER:
Feedback I want to seek from my direct report:	
Projects or tasks I want to ask about:	

QUESTIONS I WANT TO ASK

1-ON-1 PLANNER FOR TEAM MEMBERS

DATE:

CHALLENGES, OPPORTUNITIES, AND SUPPORT

Outcome and follow-up items from previous 1-on-1:	
My biggest challenge right now and ways my manager could help me:	
My biggest opportunity right now and ideas about next steps:	

DATE:

Things my manager should know but doesn't:	
Additional information I need to do my job:	
Other tasks or projects I want to talk about:	

DEVELOPMENT GOALS AND PLANNING

Review of progress toward my development goals:	
List of things I'd like to ask my manager for feedback on:	
Development area I want to focus on this week and how my manager can help me:	

FEEDBACK FOR MY MANAGER

Reinforcing feedback I want to give to help my manager improve:	
Redirecting feedback I want to give to help my manager improve:	

COACHING QUESTIONS TOOL

Use these open-ended questions with your 1-on-1 prep worksheet:

To Gauge the Team Member's Engagement Level

Personal

- How are you feeling about your role?
- In what ways do you feel like you're growing, or not growing, in your role? What makes you say that?
- What interests you about the project(s) you're currently working on, and why?
- What is your favorite/least favorite thing about your work right now?
- How do you think that least favorite thing affects your overall performance?
- What's working well for you in your current position?
- What would you like to see change?
- In what ways does your current position allow you to use your skills and talents?
- Which areas make you feel like you're stuck or unable to reach your full potential?
- What do you think you could be doing differently?
- If you could work on anything for the next month, what would it be?
- What's one thing that could make your work more satisfying, and why?
- Which areas would you like more feedback on?

Team

- How would you describe the personality of the team? What sort of person would work well here? What sort of person would add something we're currently missing?
- How could we improve our teamwork?
- Is there anything you'd like to see change about the team, and if so, why?

Manager

- In what ways do you feel supported, or not supported, by me?
- What am I doing or not doing to help you succeed?
- In what ways can I clear the path for you to make your job more interesting or less complicated?

To Draw Out an Issue

- Can you share some of the details around that particular issue?
- What was that experience like for you?
- How did that affect you?
- What do you think caused that to happen?

To Coach a Team Member to Solve a Problem

- What's your number-one problem right now?
- What have you tried so far?
- What ideas can you bring in from past successes?
- What haven't you tried yet?

To Support Career Development

- What are some of the work projects you're most proud of, and what do you think you might want to do next?
- What are two to three new skills you'd like to learn on the job? What about those skills interests you?
- What other roles could you see yourself playing down the line? Or what areas would you like to explore?
- If you were to create your ideal position, how would it differ from what you are currently doing?

To Learn About Challenges

- What is the biggest challenge you are currently facing? How can I help with that?
- At what point in the past week were you most frustrated with or discouraged by your work? What can I do to help you manage that?
- What are your biggest concerns about your current project(s)?

To Learn More About a Project

- What aspect of this project has been particularly interesting for you?
- What frustrates you about the project?
- What can I do to make things more manageable?
- What do you think I should know about the project, but might not?

To Check In Regarding a Change

- What concerns do you have about this change that haven't been addressed?
- What's going well and not so well with the new situation? Why do you think this might be happening?
- How is the new situation affecting your work? What could be getting in the way of you being effective?

To Promote Continuity Between 1-on-1s

- What progress have you made on the next steps we discussed last time?
- In our last 1-on-1, you mentioned that you'd like to grow in X. How has that been going?
- What development areas do you want to work on in the coming weeks?

To Break Out of 1-on-1s That Feel Ineffective or in a Rut

- What would you like to see change about these discussions? How could we make them more useful for you?
- I'm trying to make our 1-on-1s better and would appreciate your honest feedback. What did you like about our 1-on-1s and what can I do better?
- What is one thing I can stop, start, or continue doing to make these 1-on-1s more valuable?

Take a moment to review this practice, and note the insights that most resonated with you.

_____

_____

_____

_____

_____

_____

_____

_____

Jot down two to three action items you want to commit to.

_____

_____

_____

_____

_____

_____

_____

_____

SET UP YOUR TEAM TO GET RESULTS

I once worked at a luxury hotel in Paris that prided itself on extraordinary customer service. Whenever a VIP would visit, the staff took extra care to set the dinner tables perfectly. They had years of experience and knew their jobs inside and out. But invariably, after the waiters had set a VIP's table, the supervisor would stop by. She would study everything, then reposition a champagne flute. A minute later, the assistant manager would show up and refold a linen napkin. The staff members would glance at each other as management corrected their work. But it wasn't over. The general manager would then stroll from his top-floor office to the VIP table. After a moment of reflection, he would rearrange the centerpiece!

After a while, the staff learned not to bother with getting the placements perfect—they knew management would do it themselves. By taking over and doing the work, these hotel leaders unwittingly sabotaged their long-term success (unless their goal was to have several layers of management adjust forks every night). Their team members grew indifferent and even resentful. They had little incentive to bring their best ideas and skills when management would simply override them anyway.

—VICTORIA

I'm always surprised how many people come to work every day and have no idea *why* they're doing what they're doing. If people are doing their jobs solely because their boss told them to, it sucks engagement right out of a team.

COMMON MINDSET	EFFECTIVE MINDSET
I tell team members what to do and how to do it.	I help team members get clear about the "why" behind the "what" and support them in the "how."

You often get promoted because of your stellar results. As the new manager, you start to build trust and rapport with your new team when, suddenly, you hit a snag. That's when the common mindset above kicks in: telling people what to do and often even more deadly, resorting to your comfort zone to do it yourself—after all, you know how to produce results. It seems faster, more controllable, and guaranteed to succeed.

But the common mindset shuts down team creativity and ownership (think of the hotel staff in Victoria's story), places a huge burden on the manager, and destroys trust. In this scenario, the boss has to know all the answers, oversee every detail, and crack the whip to make sure it gets done. I would know—I spent quite a few years with this mindset and had to consciously break myself of it. It just doesn't work long term (and in my case, even short term!). As chief marketing officer, I caught myself peering over my employees' shoulders to help choose which type of ribbon to use on a mail piece (satin, obviously). At one point, I was so focused on ribbons that one afternoon a newer employee walked up to me and asked if I had more ribbon. I sarcastically responded, "Sure. A whole roll, right here in my pocket." To my horror, he believed me. I had set the expectation that the CMO of a global professional-services company would personally manage ribbon inventory. It became a ludicrous lesson in micromanagement.

If leaders tell their teams exactly how to debug the code, write the grant application, or issue ribbon—they'll be doing the same thing a year from now. It's not scalable. If you're not delegating (which also involves teaching, coaching, and advising), you're an individual producer masquerading as a leader. You may think nobody knows. In fact, they do . . . everyone knows.

In contrast, the effective mindset helps your team become invested in decisions and understand the big picture behind the daily grind. But it does require an ongoing investment of time, patience, and maturity. Great leaders plan goals *with* their teams rather than *for* them, and delegate tasks without abandoning or micromanaging. They shift from telling team members what to do, to aligning their work to greater purposes and supporting their efforts.

Let me share a somewhat humbling story of how my successor transformed the level of engagement in the Marketing division after me through adherence to this principle. For nearly a decade, I decided the budget and goals for our Marketing team somewhat unilaterally. Every year, I would sit with my own boss, door closed, discuss the team goals, develop a budget, then dole out resources to the team as I saw fit. This worked quite well . . . because no one knew the difference. I centralized power and decision making at my level and above, and although I discussed tactics with my team, I ultimately decided what would be approved and at what funding level.

When my successor took on the role, he—like all new bosses—set out to create his own cultural standards and processes. One of the first things he did was open up the budget to his direct reports. He set the priorities with his boss, and then, unlike my process, he sat down with his team, discussed the goals of the division, asked for their input, and then built the budget transparently with them, which developed a much higher level of engagement and empowerment around that process.

Then he took it a step further. Once he knew the budget allocated for their projects, he turned over portions of the budget to them, and *they* decided how to invest it for the highest return. Now the social media manager had his own budget and decided how to spend it. So did the marketing automation manager, the creative services director, and so on.

As I reflect on my approach versus his, I've been inspired to trust my team members more and hoard information less. If I had a redo, I would have been less fearful about turning over some control and more interested in the team's insights, because they were closer to the actual work that needed to get done to achieve the goals. My successor's process was high involvement, high commitment—versus my process, which was no involvement, compulsory commitment.

A few years ago, I was working with a franchisee of an international fast-food chain who faced a difficult decision after Sweden passed tax reforms. He either had to increase revenues, or cut costs by letting people go. At first, he tried to motivate his people to do more with extrinsic motivators like performance bonuses. But that didn't have much of an effect, and it looked like he would have to reduce his workforce across ten stores.

After an in-depth discussion, we brought the entire staff together, and he shared the "why" behind what was going on: the tax calculation had changed, and stores needed to be more profitable to save jobs. Together, the teams collaborated on the goals they needed to achieve and the specific behaviors they would adopt to meet those goals. The owner made himself available to support the staff in the "how."

Almost immediately, things changed. Crew members made improvements and reduced costs. Management removed obstacles that got in the way or rearranged resources to fit current needs. And the results skyrocketed! Soon these ten stores were outperforming others and met the goals they'd set, saving many jobs. But it only happened once the owner and his management team changed their thinking first, then shared what was going on and stepped back.

—VICTORIA

SETTING UP YOUR TEAM SO YOU CAN WORK *ON* THE SYSTEM

Dr. Stephen R. Covey taught a related concept that inspires and haunts me daily. He described two types of leadership responsibilities, both valuable: working "*in* the system" (doing things right) and working "*on* the system" (doing the right things). Working in the system is the daily job, tasks, meetings, and projects to keep the business going. Working on the system includes higher-level strategic direction, visioning, and systems alignment. Effective leaders balance their focus.

Working in the system isn't a bad thing. It's necessary: rolling up your sleeves and getting the work done with your colleagues. But too often, leaders still acting as individual producers are *solely* working in the system. Interestingly, some leaders stay working in the system to find validation and see tangible results from their efforts. This sometimes happens when their own leaders aren't engaged or providing them with any feedback.

If you want to develop empowerment, buy-in, and skills for the future, you have to work *on* the system. That means focusing on long-term strategy, ensuring the right people are in the right roles, and clarifying the vision for the future.

Again, we work both ways; but asking yourself *when* can be invaluable for both you and your team. It's a delicate balance, and great leaders constantly assess where they're spending their time.

This mental check has helped me move out of my do-it-for-them micromanagement tendencies. I ask myself continually, "Am I *in*, or am I *on*?" Sometimes I'm in: focusing on quality, immediate results. Working on the system is tougher. It forces me to think longer term. Am I delegating strategically so that I have enough time to build capacity for the future? What does six, twelve, eighteen months look like for the team and me? Am I developing strengths and confidences in myself and my team so we can all move up?

This practice will help you resist landing short-term gains at the expense of building long-term capability. By clarifying goals and delegating effectively, your team will know exactly what they need to do to win—and you should feel some much-needed relief from having to shoulder the burden on your own.

I always tried to have the approach that everyone on my team should be able to have my job in the future. Maybe they don't want to or choose to, but that's my goal: I'm growing future directors of learning and development.

Some managers might feel threatened by that mindset. I'm always training my team to succeed in their current roles, while also preparing them to take on the next one, and using delegation as a tool to do so.

You have a lot of big goals as a leader, and that can be a little bit scary. You might feel it's all on your shoulders, but you can train everyone on your team to carry increasing weight.

—VICTORIA

SKILL 1: ALIGN GOALS TO ORGANIZATIONAL PRIORITIES

By focusing on the right priorities, you can achieve amazing results; but with the wrong focus, you can take the ship down.

Can you answer these questions?

1. What are your team's top three priorities?
2. What are your boss's top three priorities?
3. How does your team contribute to your organization's priorities?

   . . . and can everyone (anyone?) on your team answer these questions too?

Some leaders struggle to narrow their focus to a few key priorities. They try to do everything. Others, like me, have no problem focusing—but not always on the right thing. As a marketing leader, I was occasionally more invested in a strategy than my own boss was, and my intense focus became a source of frustration for him. No one ever accused me of lacking focus—but was I focused on the highest-leverage activities for the company?

Through this and other experiences, I learned to check if my priorities were aligned with my leader's. That's where my credibility really came from. When he saw me using my hard-earned influence to achieve his top priorities, I was unstoppable; but when I was off—by guessing, following a personal preference, or leading out without permission—I found myself at odds with him. That wasn't where I wanted to be.

Don't guess what your team should focus on. You can run with your strengths, take on projects you're passionate about, and dream up interesting initiatives—as long as they align with the organization's priorities. Make sure that your team is focused on what your boss wants to accomplish.

If you haven't discussed your team's goals with your leader, request a meeting: "Would you be willing to spend twenty minutes going over our team goals for the upcoming month/quarter/year?"

Make sure you understand the why behind the goals too. If you're not bought in, your team certainly won't be.

—TODD

If you can't meet with your manager, don't use that as an excuse to not align your work with their priorities. I'm not able to meet with my boss as often as we'd like. So I've gotten into the habit of emailing him once a week with something like "Five things you may need to know." I make it clear and to the point, always bulleted. Included are highlights of my team's focus and decisions I've made that I need him to know about. Unless he responds otherwise, I charge forward. Nine times out of ten, he simply writes back, "Thanks." That's enough to make sure we're aligned.

This process may work in your culture too. It allows you to stay connected to extremely busy leaders and keep them abreast of the most important things going on. This email update isn't intended to replace a 1-on-1, but you might be surprised how it keeps you oriented toward your leader's true north.

CHOOSE A FEW MEASURABLE GOALS

Limit your goals to the most important. If you have discretion about setting your goals (versus receiving them from your leader), involve your team in formulating them. Not only will they be doing the work, they'll often have a perspective you (and other leaders) don't.

You will likely have more great ideas than your team has the capacity to execute. A lot of leaders overestimate how many goals their team can pack into any given period, insisting *everything* is important. But humans are hardwired to do only a few things at a time with excellence. Ideally, your team should focus on no more than three important goals at a time.

Of course, this is easier said than done. You can't walk around saying, "We're only doing three things, sorry." There's a careful balance between keeping your boss happy with your team's performance and keeping your team from burning out. When discussing your team's priorities, consider having a transparent conversation with your manager about this balance. Any mature leader will understand this challenge, because they've been there as well.

If your boss hands down unrealistic or too many goals, push back on them respectfully. Consider saying, "I'm sorry, but I know that having so many competing goals is going to crush my people. We will work hard, but this isn't setting our team up for success in the long term, and I'm concerned it might cause some to burn out and leave." That's a bold statement, and it may take a lot of courage to say it. You have to earn your way into that, with a reputation of saying yes to a lot of things in the past, stretching, and using your resourcefulness and initiative.

If your leader insists on keeping a dozen goals, ask if you can stagger them in a hierarchy of importance. Prioritize them so you can focus on two or three at a time.

Your goals must be specific and measurable. They usually contain a starting line, a finish line, and a deadline, which we express as: **From X to Y by When**.

For example:

- Increase customer-satisfaction scores from 88 percent to 90 percent by January 31.
- Reduce project timelines from 48 to 38 days by the end of the fiscal year.
- Cut costs from $1.4 million to $1.2 million by the end of the quarter.

Setting Stretch Goals

Sometimes we set stretch goals that are great in theory, without clarifying what we can do to make them happen.

Based on the success of the corporate headquarters, our local office once instituted a goal that our sales teams spend ten hours a week meeting face-to-face with clients. We had never measured this on our team before, so we essentially went from 0 to 10.

It was a great goal statistically—but our team simply wasn't ready yet, and it became demotivating because the bar was way too high. No one runs a marathon with one day's notice. It would have been better if we had said (both to the corporate office and the team), "Hey, first quarter, let's start with three hours per week and then grow from there." Additionally, we should have discussed how to get those hours with clients. What new activities would we need to undertake to reach that goal? What new skills would we need to maximize those hours with clients once they were secured?

If people don't understand what to do with their goal or how they can influence it, take it one step back and say, "What can we do to actually affect it?" And then put those behaviors as your initial goal. Once those are mastered, you can move up to the next step toward the stretch goal.

—VICTORIA

USE A SCOREBOARD

Chris McChesney, lead author of FranklinCovey's bestselling book *The 4 Disciplines of Execution*, says, "People play differently when they're keeping score."

A scoreboard can help people see where they are against their goals, relative to where they should be. It can be a fun way to motivate people—and keep your goals top of mind. Without it, you risk falling into business as usual.

Here are four key traits of an effective scoreboard:

- **Simple.** While you may track a lot of data as a leader, the team only needs to see the goal and the few metrics they chose that drive it. You should be able to tell in a glance if you're winning or losing: green/yellow/red bars, emojis, speedometers, etc. Depending on your situation, you might be tracking the team's overall performance toward the goal or breaking it down by individual.

- **Visible.** Out of sight, out of mind. No one will care about winning if the scoreboard is stuck in a drawer. Post it in a high-traffic place. Make it everyone's screensaver or desktop image.

- **Updated frequently.** Nothing is more demotivating than announcing new goals with fanfare and designing a scoreboard that gets everyone's attention . . . and then not keeping it updated. You must install systems to continually update the data in real time as much as possible (especially if you're tracking individual performance).

- **As engaging as your culture allows.** You don't want your team scoreboard to get lost in a sea of emails, files, or even other goal scoreboards. Make your scoreboard attention-grabbing. Capitalize on inside jokes in your company's culture. We once hired a cartoonist to produce a comic strip every day of an especially important campaign. Another scoreboard featured our leaders slowly sinking into quicksand unless our metrics improved. If at all possible, make it fun.

Remember that scoreboards can be inspiring—or shaming. If you're measuring individual performance, be thoughtful, careful, and aware about how the people on the bottom of the list react. Do they feel motivated to rise up the scoreboard—or are they just getting pummeled at the bottom? Know your culture. Tracking individual performance publicly could be demotivating when people didn't sign up for a role that suddenly has a competitive or comparative aspect to it. Use good judgment.

Engaging Part-Time and Contract Workers with a Scoreboard

During my school years, I worked part-time as a waitress. I came in every second weekend to work in the restaurant and, as you might expect, no one explained anything to me about the goals. But they did have a big bulletin board above the staff entrance where I could see exactly how many sales they'd had against their goal and whatever they were measuring at the time: glasses of wine, appetizers, etc.

The goals were so clear even for me, who just came in a few times a month. I could see, "Wow, I can influence that number on my shift," and "Look, my shift scored much better this week than last week."

That experience made me realize that a simple scoreboard can help team members who work less often feel engaged too.

Many leaders don't see that power of having a great scoreboard. It can be your "extra arm," reaching out to all those people you may not have time to connect with. Create something clear and simple to get your entire team on board. And like the restaurant's scoreboard, it should be the centerpiece of your workplace, not in the corner.

—VICTORIA

HOLD TEAM ACCOUNTABILITY MEETINGS

Without accountability, teams will lose focus on what's important—it's just human nature. The urgencies of daily activity will soon take over, while the scoreboard collects dust.

Accountability should have a rhythm to it. Bring the team together regularly for brief team accountability meetings, dedicated to moving the needle on the scoreboard.

Take note: These are *not* staff meetings, where you share updates, make announcements, or introduce new hires. They're also not 1-on-1 meetings, as discussed in Practice 2. During accountability meetings (which are very short and even done while standing), the agenda is simple: team members review the scoreboard, account for the commitments they made last week, and make new commitments for the coming week.

Here are some best practices:

- Don't discuss anything unrelated to your goals, the scoreboard, or your commitments. This takes some discipline—conversation has a tendency to spin out, so limit the discussion to the commitments as they relate to the scoreboard.

- Keep the meeting as short as possible, ten to twenty minutes max. Contrary to popular belief, I don't think people hate meetings— but they do hate unproductive, unfocused, agendaless meetings that waste time. They like meetings where stuff gets done, that start and end on time, and that have a clear purpose.

- Have a consistent agenda. The purpose of an accountability meeting is always the same: moving the metrics on the scoreboard. Each person reports on their commitments from the previous week and then commits to one or two actions in the next week that will bring the team closer to the goal. These commitments must represent a specific deliverable supporting the agreed-upon goals and be achievable within the person's ability and authority.

- Clear the path. Too few leaders recognize that an important part of their role is to make their team members' jobs easier. That doesn't mean you're doing their job for them; rather, you're clearing obstacles that only your title, stature, tenure, or experience can tackle. What might take you ten minutes could take them two weeks. Sometimes less mature leaders are unwilling or unable to use their influence. With time, you'll learn when to do it (and, just as important, when not to). Clearing the path isn't always fun; sometimes you have to bulldoze through bureaucracy and handle uncomfortable conversations, but you'll earn the respect of your team.

- In advance, consider assigning a member of the group to facilitate each meeting. You may need to show them how to run it, but this further moves accountability to the team.

As simple as these meetings seem, they build powerful momentum toward achieving your goals, keeping everyone on the same page, and working toward the same big goals together. But your team will only take them as seriously as you do. If you cancel them frequently or stay glued to your phone during them, the team will check out as well. Hold them regularly, keep them focused, and model their importance. Instead of a vague outcome they can't influence, your team will feel personally accountable for a winning result that's within their power.

Short. Fast-paced. Standing. Go get 'em.

SKILL 2: DELEGATE

When I was twenty years old, I worked at the Florida headquarters of a U.S. presidential campaign. (Fill in the candidate of your choice so we can stay friends.) Before a big rally in Tampa, the campaign manager tasked me with creating a balloon arch for the stage backdrop, an image that would be broadcast on the evening news to millions of people. I had no idea how to create a balloon arch—surely there was a science to it!—so I chased down the campaign manager to ask some follow-up questions. He said, "I don't know, Scott, you figure it out. I trust you."

I remember thinking, "Why would you possibly trust me to do this alone? I don't know what I'm doing!" To him, the balloon arch was one of a thousand tasks in his purview. To me, it was the most important project I'd ever had.

I ended up putting together a balloon arch that wasn't too shabby, but I've thought about this incident many times since then: Was the campaign manager empowering me or abandoning me? Was he showing confidence in me? Or was the whole thing super trivial and I didn't realize it?

Ultimately, it was a combination of things. I *was* overthinking it, and he knew me well enough to show confidence in me that I didn't have in myself. Interestingly, I'm employing his same tactic thirty years later. When a competent employee asks me for something that I know they can do themself, I'll usually push it right back to them, because the growth that moment builds in them is lifelong.

I've come to see delegating like taking a road trip. **The abandoning leader** wants to be driven to the destination with as little involvement as possible. This leader delegates as a way of off-loading work onto someone else. With a blanket, pillow, and headphones, this leader is curled up in the passenger's seat asleep, not offering to help with navigation or passing the time with conversation—and certainly not paying for gasoline. The driver feels overworked, unmotivated, and deeply resentful.

The micromanager delegates as a way of controlling things from the passenger's seat. They expect the driver to do everything the way they would and dictate the smallest details: "Watch out for that car in the next lane! Use your turn signal now!" The driver feels irritated and distracted. The micromanager knows (or has been told) that they should let the other person drive, but wishes they were actually driving.

The empowering leader delegates by willingly inviting the team member to take the wheel. They find ways to help the driver, like troubleshooting the GPS, finding a radio station, and putting gas in the car. This leader focuses on supporting the driver, not directing their every move. At the end of the trip, the driver asks, "Where are we going next?"

HOW TO DELEGATE EFFECTIVELY

In the previous scenario, we can imagine the empowering leader's driver as being committed and even excited about the trip; the abandoning leader's driver as indifferent or even resentful; and the micromanager's driver as ready to rebel or quit at the earliest opportunity.

How you handle delegation affects your team's growth, engagement, and motivation. Consider using the following process to delegate effectively:

Define the project. If you don't understand a project, you can't delegate it properly. What are the objectives and deadlines? What skills will someone need to complete the task? How much time will it take? Have you defined what success looks like and identified key metrics to pursue? If you're not clear on what success looks like, you can be sure no one else is either.

This is such an easy step to skip. Even the most seasoned business leaders benefit from asking themselves how they'll measure success. Sometimes all of us are tempted to launch right into the "what" and skip the "why," which is important not just to our teams but to ourselves.

Decide if the project should be delegated. Especially with first-time managers, delegating can be a slippery slope. You might be tempted to hoard things, because you want to own them and get them done according to your standards. On the other hand, if you overdelegate, you can get a reputation of not doing any of the work. Be deliberate about delegating authentically.

Some leadership responsibilities should never be delegated, and this depends heavily on the cultural norms of your organization. Typically, as a leader, if it's overly complicated or requires great sensitivity, you should own it. Don't delegate the hard stuff and keep the easy, fun stuff—the opposite, in fact. You need to be willing to take on the tough people, strategies, and systems issues, because in all likelihood, you're responsible for those problems as the leader. You also have to build a reputation of rolling up your sleeves with your employees. If your team sees that you're occasionally willing to sit on the floor packing boxes, they won't accuse you of delegating through neglect or delegating to get out of work.

I try to delegate to make the best use of my time, not to pawn things off on my team. However, occasionally I will dip into lower-level tasks to remind my team that I'm not above that work and we're in this together. It's a culture-building moment. As a leader, I shouldn't do everything . . . and I am willing to do anything. I make sure that of all the complaints people have about me, no one will say, "Scott can't handle the tough issue" or "He delegated the crappy stuff to us."

Decide whom to delegate the project to. For each team member you are considering delegating a task to, think through this quick checklist:

- Do they have the time?
- Is this something they've expressed interest in?
- Do they have the skills needed? How much coaching will be required?
- Do they typically meet deadlines?

- Will they benefit from working on this task by learning a new skill or improving an existing one?
- Will they work well with the other stakeholders?
- Is there any chance that giving this person this task will be seen as unfair by the team?
- Will they see it as a compliment and reward, or as a burden?

Scope the project with the team member. Even if you have a vision for a project in your head, you can't assume it's clear in other people's minds.

People often are afraid to ask questions of their manager for fear it will make them look incapable. Then they lack clarity, leading to procrastination, or worse, failure to deliver the true end in mind.

Blaine Lee, a renowned executive coach and author of *The Power Principle*, said that nearly all, if not all, conflict results from mismatched, unfulfilled, or violated expectations—whether it's negotiating rates with your childcare provider or setting vacation schedules with your team. Think about your last discussions where some conflict arose: If you had been clearer about your needs and wants, and listened more closely to others', could you have prevented the snowball of confusion and resulting conflict?

You must clarify expectations, sometimes even to the point of absurdity. It's your job to say things like, "This would be a great time to ask any clarifying questions. Everything is on the table. Nothing is undiscussable—even uncomfortable questions."

Clarifying expectations is a leadership competency. It may take extra effort, diplomacy, and a stretch beyond your comfort level. When a leader delegates and gets back a poor result, it is usually the leader's responsibility. I've learned to minimize confusion up front by setting clear expectations. The clearer you describe the purpose, vision, and expected results, the less you have to manage the process itself. In other words, explain the "why" and let the team determine the "how."

EVERYONE DESERVES A GREAT MANAGER

The main obstacle is often taking the time to clarify expectations. But if you don't do this, you will find yourself in the perpetual cycle of constantly fixing, cleaning up, and doing it yourself.

Here's a framework to delegate work in a way that reveals the "why" and creates clarity.

- **State the why.** Clarify why this project is important.
- **State the what.** Clarify what success looks like and how success will be measured.
- **Discuss the how.**
  - Guidelines: the standards and conditions that must be met, including the deadline.
  - Resources: people, budget, tools, etc.
  - Accountability: how to track progress and be accountable. You might want to meet in person, get a status report over email, etc.
  - Impact: define the benefits if the project is completed (and the consequences if the work is not).

Don't be tempted to rely on your memory alone. Prevent misunderstandings and lost accountability through clear note-taking and a record of assignments.

Support. You've delegated the assignment. Now you can put your feet up on your desk and relax. Just kidding. Apart from all your other work, you'll need to support your team member in their new assignment, calibrated to their experience and confidence. They might have to go through rough patches that might stretch their competencies. Remember, it's healthy for your team to make some mistakes—that's how people learn. Even when you've been enormously clear, there are going to be less-than-perfect results as people level up their skillsets and knowledge.

One of my first leaders had a cultural imperative: we were pre-forgiven for mistakes. This encouraged brainstorming and appropriate risk-taking. We knew that if we made a mistake, we weren't going to get in trouble. Our responsibility was not to take overly risky measures and tell him as soon as things went sideways.

To further support us, he empowered us frontline employees to make customer-service decisions up to $500 on the spot, and he would never second-guess our decision. More than $500, and we had to involve him. That empowerment unleashed people's creativity. Because it was such a precious gift, people rarely used it. We didn't want to disappoint him. He gave so much latitude that we took less than we otherwise would have. We were so appreciative of the trust that we never wanted to violate it.

Establishing a pre-forgiveness culture means trusting your team with a level of empowerment. They're going to make some mistakes, and they're pre-forgiven. In exchange, they can't be cavalier. They don't work outside established bounds. You widened the lane, so there's no reason for them to go off-road. They have to report if something is failing so you can help them get back on track.

Pre-forgiveness lightens the air. This level of trust is rare, especially with new leaders who are usually focused on buttoning up and tightening down, which leaves little room for growth.

Pre-forgiveness in your culture might look different. And if someone violates it, you might pull back. But most people will respond the way we did: gratitude drove respect, which drove judicious thinking, which drove better client results and sales growth.

If your team member is struggling with the assigned task, check in during your 1-on-1s. Look to Practice 4 for insights on how to give feedback. If they come back with an underwhelming result, take the time to repaint a clear vision of success. To prevent a repeat, agree to check in more frequently this time.

A FINAL NOTE: WORK HARD, CELEBRATE BIG

Like most sales organizations, FranklinCovey has an annual kickoff meeting at the beginning of the fiscal year. This is a time to celebrate successes, lick any wounds, share lessons learned, and set goals for the coming year. As you might expect, these conferences can devolve into a litany of speeches, career posturing, and death by PowerPoint. Lots of useful information, but it can feel like overload and less celebratory than was intended.

One year in particular, we were on the cusp of launching a global refresh of *The 7 Habits of Highly Effective People* work session, a live multiday program for professionals to learn and implement the contents of the book. In the coming months, we would simultaneously launch the product in multiple languages across 170 cities worldwide. A massive undertaking that required unprecedented effort, focus, and discipline.

In preparation for unveiling the product to our internal associates, the Marketing division calculated how many people worldwide had experienced the *7 Habits* in total through live work sessions, online learning, blended learning, podcasts, webinars, print and ebooks, and keynote speeches, in what was for many a life-changing experience. Our research showed it was more than thirty-seven million people, at the time. Think about that: we had directly, positively, sustainably im-pacted the lives of *thirty-seven million people* for the better. It was both humbling and validating.

We couldn't just slap that number on a slide and call it a day. It needed to be visual and visceral.

As an executive vice president, I'd been afforded a thirty-minute keynote presentation in front of the entire company during the conference. So on the morning of my speech, after planning and trial runs, our team stealthily wheeled fourteen confetti cannons (the size of riding lawn mowers) into the hotel ballroom and hid them under tablecloths, ready to be deployed at a precisely agreed-upon time. This required intense coordination with the hotel management. The fire marshal had to inspect the pressurized air tanks, and the cleanup crew was standing by.

These fourteen cannons were loaded with thirty-seven million pieces of crepe-paper confetti in the shape of 3 inch-size mini people. We weren't just going to report our impact. We were going to *show* it in a way no one would ever forget. When was the last time you experienced thirty-seven million of anything?

Interestingly, up until moments before my speech, another executive who knew the confetti plan implored me not to do it. He felt the silliness was going to diminish my credibility, and the other executives would not appreciate it the way I envisioned. This particular colleague asked that I reconsider my plan, even as I was preparing to walk onstage. He had my best interests in mind, but I had calibrated the upside and downsides and wasn't turning back. I felt so compelled about the value of the visual to paint a magnificent vision not just of what we had achieved, but of what was possible in the future, that I was willing to take the risk to my own brand. (Plus it's hard to return loaded confetti cannons.)

It was me. I told him not to do it.

—TODD

I thanked him for his counsel, walked onstage, and unleashed the most spectacular indoor confetti downpour anyone has seen short of winning a World Series. It was a twelve-minute nonstop barrage of confetti. You could bury a body in it. Otherwise buttoned-up people were on the floor making snow angels and throwing handfuls of confetti in the air.

This demonstration wasn't merely confetti for confetti's sake. It was a carefully orchestrated visual and emotional strategy to ingrain in everyone's mind the power and reach our brand had across thirty-seven million people. Imagine what it would have looked like if we had demonstrated the next thirty-seven million with confetti. (No, we didn't do this—we do have an environmental conscience. And yes, it was recycled. No paper dolls were harmed in this display.) Frankly, not everyone reacted the same way. I'm guessing some people thought it was frivolous, and others truly thought it was life-affirming, with hundreds in the middle.

When the last confetti had fallen, I calmly and deliberately explained the "why" behind the "what." I challenged everybody to visualize a client who they knew had been impacted by the 7 *Habits*—to picture the person, the leader, the line worker, the teacher, the receptionist. For every person they could visualize in their mind, I asked them to pick up a piece of confetti and put it in their wallet, purse, briefcase, or planner—whatever they carried with them day to day. And every time they came across it, I wanted it to serve as a reminder of our mission and impact.

For weeks post-conference, FranklinCovey colleagues from around the world were texting and emailing me photos of confetti falling out of their pockets. People were finding confetti in their bathrooms, in their underwear. Bits and pieces of confetti had stuck around, which was amazing because it unintentionally reinforced the visualization of our impact. I couldn't have planned a longer shelf life for any presentation had I tried.

I found confetti in my shoe after traveling back to Stockholm!
—VICTORIA

And nearly a decade on, whenever I visit our offices in Japan, China, Brazil, Portugal, or Mexico, someone will inevitably take out their wallet, pull out a barely identified piece of confetti, and tell me what the message meant to them. They're choosing to keep these reminders through their own initiatives; I've done nothing to follow up with it since the conference.

Not everybody can shoot confetti cannons, but that's okay: Big celebrations don't necessarily need big budgets. What's your scalable equivalent to celebrate your successes? Thoughtful recognition and creative surprises can make a decades-long impact.

Often in focused, hardworking companies, we get in ruts. It's a mistake to think if we celebrate, we're gloating or losing our edge. Of course, don't celebrate *everything*, because then it doesn't mean anything. But when you've done the hard work of this practice—focusing on your most critical important goals, aligning your work to achieve them, and accomplishing this as a team—I truly believe that you cannot celebrate enough.

People want to have fun in their jobs. They want to feel appreciated. They want to look forward to coming to work. So after you've worked your heart out to achieve a goal, take some time to celebrate.

Take a moment to review this practice, and note the insights that most resonated with you.

_____

_____

_____

_____

_____

_____

_____

Jot down two to three action items you want to commit to.

_____

_____

_____

_____

_____

_____

_____

CREATE A CULTURE OF FEEDBACK

In college, I was one of the highest-tipped waiters at the Sunset Grill in Winter Park, Florida. I developed a system for delivering the absolute fastest service. Because I've always had a pretty good memory, I'd simply take my tables' orders without notes, race back to the kitchen, and let the cooks know exactly what I needed . . . ahead of everyone else.

With this speedy—albeit somewhat selfish—system, my tables were enjoying their desserts when other customers were still waiting for their soup. In the restaurant business, it's all about turning over the tables. My customers loved me, and I had the tips to prove it. But every time I exited the kitchen, I left chaos in my wake.

Eventually, one of my friends, a fellow waiter, was promoted to manager. One day he was serving fettuccine Alfredo with the rest of us; the next day he was our boss.

The first item on his managerial to-do list was to crack down on my chaos. I viscerally remember the moment he sat me down after the last customer had cleared out, and said, "Scott, I need to see a marked improvement in your teamwork." Then he took out an index card, wrote down what he'd just said word for word, and handed me the card.

I was shocked. I thought, "Who the hell do you think you are? You were my buddy three days ago, and now you want to see a 'marked' improvement?"

How many of us can remember *the exact moment* we received some difficult feedback? I don't think it's an overstatement to say that feedback is often traumatic, for both the giver and the receiver. And yet Dr. Stephen R. Covey wrote, "One of the greatest gifts you can give another human being is constructive feedback on a blind spot they never knew they had. It's a great disservice not to say what needs to be said just because it isn't comfortable. Care enough to give honest, accurate feedback."

Now I can appreciate that my restaurant manager had the courage to tell it to me straight. He had the right intention, but the skills in this chapter would have helped him deliver sensitive feedback without an index card.

As a leader, your job is to summon the courage and consideration to provide actionable, specific, and sometimes tough feedback to your employees. It's an art, not a science, and it's learned through repetition. It isn't just a nice-to-have skill; if you want to be an effective leader, you *must* learn to do this. Taking it a step further, we believe you don't have the right to be a leader if you're not willing to step out of your comfort zone and provide people with feedback.

When it comes to giving feedback, there are two extremes:

- **Too much courage.** This type of boss has no problem telling anybody what they think. I have fallen into this camp, and I may have even given too much feedback, too harshly, too often.

- **Too much consideration.** For this other type of person, the thought of giving someone tough feedback makes them want to throw up. So they avoid it entirely, and the problems not only persist, but grow.

Both extremes of the spectrum do their teams a disservice. With too much courage and not enough consideration, I might destroy someone's self-esteem or confidence. I don't know when to stop. I never set out to harm people, but I deliver brutally honest feedback and let the person deal with it the best they know how.

But just as damaging is too much consideration and no courage, where the leader unintentionally abandons their team. By not giving feedback at all or being too vague, they're reinforcing employees' weaknesses. The team members keep falling into the same traps that hinder their performance and growth. Failing to give feedback also damages the team's perception of the boss. If you seem to be ignoring a challenging or difficult issue, the team may see you as weak and lose confidence in your abilities.

I find that your amount of courage and consideration is situational, depending on the relationship. How long have you been managing them? Are you intimidated by the person? How mature are they? Perhaps they're older and more experienced than you. Some team members are more difficult to provide feedback to; others are more receptive to coaching.

Do you have a natural tendency: too much courage or too much consideration? Does it vary depending on the relationship?

It's a balance. You ideally want to be high in both courage and consideration in every situation and relationship.

—VICTORIA

Whatever our natural tendency, it's up to us to find the right balance.

COMMON MINDSET	EFFECTIVE MINDSET
I give feedback so I can fix people's problems.	I give *and* seek feedback to elevate the entire team.

The common manager mindset is to think of yourself as "the fixer": your team has problems, so you think it's your job to point out what they are doing wrong through feedback. In contrast, the effective mindset is all about unleashing the potential in others—including yourself, when you seek feedback.

Giving feedback comes down to motives. Your team has to know your intent is to help them develop their skills and talents. They have to feel secure and safe with you. And that doesn't happen overnight; you have to build a reservoir of trust.

Leaders provide feedback to help people see what they are not seeing. In my experience, most people (including me, perhaps even you) aren't naturally self-aware. Your team members' previous managers might not have called out what the team needed to work on in a way that built them up.

As a leader, you have blind spots too. Part of this mindset shift is being willing to let go of your ego and seek feedback from your team. This not only models the skills you want your team to practice, but helps *you* improve while creating a sense of safety around giving and receiving feedback.

People regard feedback differently based on their individual experiences, but some universal principles apply to almost everyone. Feedback matters just as much to a young employee working her first job out of college as it does to the thirty-year veteran starting to think about retirement. As you master giving and receiving feedback through practice, you'll get to a place where you can use your natural instincts to grow a culture in which constructive, well-intended thoughts flow freely in both directions. Everyone feels heard and respected, and performance and productivity blossom.

SKILL 1: GIVE REINFORCING FEEDBACK

Everybody wants to be valued. And you can help communicate that through reinforcing feedback.

Reinforcing feedback shouldn't be routine or formulaic. Simply be mindful of this question: "Am I reinforcing and praising the right performance at the right time for the right people?"

I'm specifically using the term "reinforcing feedback" instead of "positive feedback" to avoid just a pat on the back, a "You're awesome! Way to go! You're the best." That type of feedback is encouraging but doesn't provide specific enough information about what the person did well. Reinforcing feedback clearly communicates that a team member's behavior, attitude, or work is outstanding, and that they should keep it up. It can influence behavior change and increase engagement.

Reinforcing feedback has many purposes:

- To affirm a team member's method of solving a problem and let them know that they should keep doing it. "When you reorganized the data-gathering process, you simplified a confusing and frustrating system. Let me know if you see other opportunities to do that."

- To instill confidence in someone stretching their capacity or working on something unfamiliar. "I know you were nervous about taking on the benefits project, but I want you to know how impressed I am with your ability to get answers and figure out what you didn't know."

- To encourage a more positive culture where people don't feel taken for granted. "Before we move on to your next project, I wanted to make sure you know how much I appreciated your extra effort on the last project."

- To reassure someone developing a new skill that they're making progress. "I know you may be feeling like you're in over your head with this project, but I'm confident from what I've seen so far that you are headed in the right direction and will make this work."

- To help a new team member feel recognized and appreciated. "In the few short weeks you've been on the team, we have all been so impressed with the difference you are making. Your willingness and courage to diplomatically ask why we are doing things a certain way has us rethinking some old processes."

- To reinforce and point out a skill or a talent that the individual may have not noticed themself. "Yesterday when you greeted the guests at the door rather than waiting for them to reach the reception desk, you made a difference in a noticeable service you provided them. I could see just how welcomed you made them feel."

Ditch the Sandwich

As leaders, we're trained to point out what's not right and to fix things. We often think of positive feedback as a way to "sandwich" negative feedback: start with a slice of positive feedback, slather on a thick layer of negative feedback, and then top it off with another piece of positive feedback.

Many managers also consider reinforcing feedback to be a pep talk or something you do to keep a positive atmosphere. But reinforcing feedback is business-critical. It's how you develop and grow your team.

—TODD

High-performing teams are nearly six times more likely to share reinforcing feedback than average teams, according to behavioral scientists Marcial Losada and Emily Heaphy. They also discovered that low-performing teams share nearly twice as much negative feedback as average-performing teams.* Reinforcing feedback is a performance-enhancing substance that's not addictive and costs nothing.

CONSIDER THIS ⑦

Vote for Behavior

A friend pointed out to me once that every time you pick a product from the shelf at the supermarket, you are casting your vote for the supermarket to stock that particular product. I try to see giving reinforcing feedback in the same way: you're

---

* Losada, M., & Heaphy, E. (2004). "The Role of Positivity and Connectivity in the Performance of Business Teams." *American Behavioral Scientist*, 47(6), 740–765. doi:10.1177/0002764203260208.

voting for the behavior you want to see on your team. So next time you see someone on your team getting it right, rather than just thinking to yourself, "Yes, we are (finally) starting to get it right!" give that behavior "your vote." Immediately or during the next 1-on-1, share with the team member what you saw and why it makes such a difference.

—VICTORIA

HOW TO GIVE REINFORCING FEEDBACK

Studies show that while most managers think they give enough reinforcing feedback, most employees feel like they don't get enough. Consider these best practices for giving reinforcing feedback:

Find the right frequency and format. Praise is like champagne: delicious in the right context, but too much on an empty stomach and you're going to regret it. Your job instead is to notice and learn how people prefer reinforcing feedback: through email, in private, verbally, during your 1-on-1s, in public during a team meeting, to their peers, to your boss—and how often. Some people might be embarrassed by public praise; others love nothing more than looking good in the eyes of their peers. There's nothing wrong with either of these—and it's easy to accommodate.

Each member of your team will have different preferences. You might give reinforcing feedback to certain team members more frequently, if that's what especially motivates them. Be careful not to assume they have the same preference as you. The idea is to use feedback to reinforce good behavior and create a culture where it's welcome.

Praise specific behavior and describe the impact on the team, goals, or project. "Great job" isn't instructive. Help your employees know exactly what they did right so they know what to keep doing. Reinforcing feedback is even more effective when you include details about the impact of the behavior. For example, "The report you developed was phenomenal. You included data from all seven divisions, which showed that our team isn't playing favorites."

Connect the behavior to their intrinsic motivation. During your regular 1-on-1s, you've hopefully uncovered what motivates your team members and revealed their vision for long-term development. Show how their good work is helping them get there. For example, if someone wants to be promoted down the line, link their behavior to their career goals. "You were so confident presenting in last week's team meeting. Looks like your efforts to become a better public speaker are really paying off," or "You showed a lot of patience mentoring our new team hire. I can see you've been working on your leadership skills."

Listen carefully to people's response. Praise makes some people uncomfortable, and your team members' responses to reinforcing feedback might give you clues about who could use additional encouragement and confidence building. Listen for these three common responses:

- **Accepting praise:** "Thanks, I spent a lot of time simplifying the executive summary, and it's nice to hear that it helped you in the meeting." The recipient indicates that they understood the specific behavior and the impact.

- **Deflecting praise:** "It was actually Carl's idea to rewrite the executive summary, not mine." Help your team member take credit by acknowledging the deflection and pointing out their contribution and reiterating the impact. Let them know that it's okay to acknowledge that they did good work.

- **Negating praise:** "It's a miracle it even turned out halfway decent." This might indicate a deeper issue. Ask open-ended questions to identify insecurities or other concerns.

Make up for the sparse feedback many remote team members receive. If you're managing remote employees, they might be starved for feedback. Go out of your way to acknowledge their good work even more frequently than you do with your onsite team. You could even deliver some reinforcing feedback via a group email to help those working remotely feel appreciated and connected. Keep the team feeling like a team.

Giving reinforcing feedback is one of the more enjoyable leadership responsibilities. Go ahead and pop that champagne.

A colleague at our organization works remotely and does a great job, but she's been feeling very disconnected from the rest of the team. Her bosses don't know as much about her as they do about the people they see in person. I was made aware of this, so I contacted her managers to get feedback on what she does well, where she could improve, and so on. Well, I must have made a strong impression about her feeling disconnected and not getting feedback, because several of those bosses called her and poured on the reinforcing feedback. It was sincere, but it was so out of context that she texted me, "I haven't had a compliment for two years, and now I get four days of nonstop compliments? What's going on?" It was a lesson in the importance of giving consistent reinforcing feedback.

—TODD

SKILL 2: GIVE REDIRECTING FEEDBACK

During my time at Disney, my boss's style was to never let the team know where they stood. It was frustrating . . . even paralyzing. I remember lying awake nearly every night, wondering if I was going to get fired the next day.

From that experience, I decided I never wanted my team to guess where they stood with me. Unfortunately, I went a little overboard, despite having good intentions. For my first decade as a manager, my strategy was to give feedback straight: *You need to speak up. You need to learn to spell. You need to work on your hygiene.* I would give feedback the same way from one team member to another, regardless of their personality, preferences, or experience—and with little to no emotional maturity. As I mentioned in the mindset section, I went all in on the courage side. (I've since learned to deliver feedback in a more considerate and respectful way.)

Redirecting feedback is what has historically been called critical or negative feedback. However, it's easy to see how weighted that word is. It implies all sorts of thoughts that can make individual contributors break out in a cold sweat: judgment, not being good enough, letting the team down, failure, punishment, even termination.

Too often, redirecting feedback is delivered only during annual reviews—but then it's too late for the team member to do anything that might influence a more positive review. No one should be caught off guard; feedback should be given consistently, but not so often that it's suffocating.

Redirecting communicates that the employee is capable of a stronger performance with some guidance. It's feedback intended to let someone know that a behavior, an attitude, or a result needs to improve—and you believe it can. But leaders at all levels tell us that giving redirecting feedback is one of the hardest, most stressful parts of their job. If you don't do it skillfully, you can destroy your relationship with someone and the progress that might have been possible.

Just because it's difficult doesn't mean you obfuscate, spin, or avoid it. You deliver redirecting feedback because you're invested in your team. Now you might be thinking, "This person will never change," but give them the opportunity to adjust and learn. After all, failure is how we all learn. They might just surprise you.

HOW TO GIVE REDIRECTING FEEDBACK

Decide if you should give feedback. Here are a few instances where redirecting feedback is a no-brainer:

- If a team member's behavior is a serious infraction or has immediate, substantial, and recurring negative consequences.
- If you believe the team member isn't likely to correct the behavior on their own.

- If reinforcing feedback and modeling haven't worked.
- If the team member genuinely wants a lot of redirecting feedback.
- If the person's behavior is negatively impacting team performance or morale.
- If the team member has a blind spot and is not aware of their behavior or the impact it has on others.
- If the behavior is an emergency, or threatens the company or the safety of your team. (These issues are beyond the scope of this chapter, but obviously, they should be dealt with immediately in a coordinated effort with your HR department.)

As a new manager, I was asked by a peer to observe her sales calls and give feedback on how she could improve. It was with great enthusiasm that I set out to help her. I noted every little item she could possibly improve. After she finished the meeting, I gave her a list of all twenty ways to change. I obviously overwhelmed her. Only later did I realize that she was actually looking for credit for how well she was conducting her sales calls. She was devastated . . . and never asked me for feedback again.

While I accidentally created an awful experience for her that day, I learned valuable lessons from my mistake. First, pick the most important things that are within the individual's power to change, and focus on those. Second, tune in and listen to the individual you are giving feedback to, no matter if they are a manager or a peer. Third, if you are addressing a blind spot, you might need to spend more time and use very specific examples in order to help the person see what you are sharing.

—VICTORIA

You can quickly overwhelm an individual if you ask them to change more than one or two behaviors at a time. No matter how calm and accepting a person is, too much redirecting behavior can be demotivating or make you seem like you're out to get them.

As a leader, pick your battles. Don't pummel someone with feedback so that they feel like they aren't doing anything right. If you're unsure whether or not to broach the subject, consider these types of issues:

- *Is this going to cause them more embarrassment than the benefit of solving it? Is this really that important? Is this going to matter?* You might hate their messy desk, but it might not be impacting their results. Consider letting it slide so you can focus on more important issues.

- *Have I built enough trust with them?* If you've only worked with them for a short time, consider waiting until you've sufficiently communicated that you're invested in them and your intent is to help.

- *Is the negative behavior a reaction to me as a manager?* I once had an employee who would put his head down and doodle whenever he got irritated in a meeting. He made it very clear that he did not want to be involved. I was about to give him feedback, when I realized that he usually checked out as a result of what I had said or done. This won't apply in all cases, but if, for example, someone isn't speaking up in meetings, consider if you're talking the majority of the time or if you might have unintentionally embarrassed them (or shut them down) the last time they suggested an idea.

- *Can I fix this with reinforcing feedback?* If the individual sometimes models the correct behavior, try instead to offer reinforcing feedback when you see them doing it right.

- *Can I fix this by modeling the correct behavior?* If you want your team to be on time for meetings or not look at their phones, start by doing this yourself. If that's the culture you want, model it—and even occasionally exaggerate the behavior.

- *Is the person emotionally ready for feedback?* If the person is on edge or under a lot of stress, wait for a better time, if possible.

- *Is the behavior actually wrong, or is it just different from how I'd do it?* If they're getting the results you want, consider letting them continue in their preferred style.

- *Is it just my personal preference?* Be especially careful about giving feedback on subjective issues like the way someone dresses, whether they wear earphones while working, etc.

- *Is the impact serious enough to justify redirecting feedback?* If the impact is small, consider letting it slide. Some managers try to correct every small behavior and create a suffocating atmosphere.

A member of my team was talented, a lot of fun, and a pleasure to work with. But she was also unorganized, which caused her to fall behind and miss deadlines for important deliverables. She was working on a project that she turned in on time. I made a point of acknowledging her performance in an email, with several others copied. I specifically commented on how getting the information when we did made a huge difference in the outcome. I went a little overboard (but in a sincere way) whenever she completed something on time. Eventually, she worked harder and harder at hitting deadlines, and the positive feedback continued from me and from others. While she never became what I would call "extremely organized," she did start to develop a reputation as someone who followed through and could be counted on.

—TODD

Prepare. Once you've determined that a behavior requires redirecting feedback, carefully plan how, when, and where you will share your feedback, and how you will handle the response. Identify the specific behavior you've observed and its impact. Omit any judgments of the person's character and stick to the facts. When you give feedback, remember what it feels like to get feedback. It's a vulnerable moment for your team member. Be as specific as possible, and remember to exercise a balance of courage and consideration.

Plan what you'll say so you eliminate ad-libbing, which can take you down a rabbit hole. Try not to become scripted, as you may lose your humanity or authenticity. If you can, role-play the feedback session with a trusted adviser who has insights and deeper experience in this skill. In a redirecting-feedback situation, your direct report might parse every word you say for hidden meaning, so be precise in your language. I never cease to be surprised at how people will recap things

I said a decade later, word for word, when I have zero recollection. Words matter, and people remember them, so choose them carefully.

I've often found that writing down my feedback prior to delivering it allows me to:

- Assess its accuracy.
- Determine how harsh or sensitive it seems.
- Separate my emotions from the situation.
- Think through specific examples and impact.
- Ensure I'm focused on behaviors and not personality styles.

—VICTORIA

The longer you wait between letting a direct report know you're going to deliver some feedback and actually giving them feedback, the more tension they'll feel. You will create unnecessary anxiety by casually saying to a team member, "Hey, I'd like to talk to you about something tomorrow." Don't do that. Most people will fixate on all the possible negatives. Keep the interval between "I'd like to share some thoughts with you" and actually sharing the thoughts as brief as possible.

Begin the discussion by stating your intent and priming the team member to listen. Be absolutely clear that your intent is to build the team member up, in an atmosphere of trust. This way, the manager is less a bearer of bad news and more of a coach helping the employee reach their goals. "Before we begin, please know that my only intent is to help you improve on some areas so you can grow."

When someone feels defensive, hostile, or embarrassed, they have a hard time hearing anything you're saying. Before the conversation begins, I do anything I can do to reduce defensiveness. That's where I always begin. I try to avoid the word "feedback," because it freezes people up. I'll say, "Hey, I want to share some information with you." I'll put myself in their place and let them know I just received helpful insights on something I did last week. "I need to share some tough information with you. I realize that when any of us receives information that's hard to hear, it's human nature to feel defensive, at least I know I do. Please know that my only intent as your manager is to help you get better."

That seems to put us on the same level and lowers their defensiveness, because they think, "He goes through this too. I'm not being singled out." That opens up their ability to hear and trust what I'm saying.

—TODD

When giving tough feedback, I'll find that, occasionally, some employees will respond with what *I'm* doing wrong as a boss. If that's likely to happen, I say, "I'm going to give you some feedback, and I can only imagine there are some things you'd like to share with me. I'm willing to hear those at a different time, but this meeting is about providing you with feedback."

Ask the employee what they think about the particular situation. You can save a lot of time and energy by first checking if the person is already aware of their behavior. Consider opening with "How did you think the client event went last week? What do you think went well and what do you think you need to improve next time?" Or in my Sunset Grill manager's case, maybe, "Hey, Scott, I notice you're super fast at serving your tables. How do you think things are going with the kitchen and the other waiters?" If they're aware, it will be easier to give feedback. If they're not, you will need to spend more time explaining and citing examples. Be careful that the person doesn't take over the conversation from there—if you have that concern, be very specific about how you phrase that question.

Describe the specific behavior you noticed and its impact. Redirecting feedback is about behavior, not character. What you say should feel neutral and nonjudgmental so the other person doesn't feel shame or become defensive. You're keeping it professional, not making it personal. Use terms like "I noticed that . . ." and be specific about the impact.

COMMON MISTAKE	USE THIS INSTEAD
You're too passive in meetings.	I noticed you didn't say anything in our last two meetings. I'm worried we're missing input from you that might cause us to delay our product launch.
You're too reactive.	I noticed you raised your voice with the client on the call and interrupted her while she was talking. I'm concerned you will diminish your personal credibility and that we'll lose her business.

I once worked with an employee who kept getting feedback that he was unpleasant to work with. That's harsh feedback to begin with, but to make things worse, he didn't know how to fix it. No one told him the specific behaviors he could work on.

As we dug into the issue, I was able to coach him on simple things like beginning emails with a greeting instead of launching right into a request. He assumed that was wasting people's time, which is understandable. While it may sound obvious to some, I gave him simple examples like, "Hey, Tina, I hope you had a great weekend. Did you have time to look through the information I sent you?" versus "Tina, did you look through the information I sent you?" or "Sam, I know you're busy and get a ton of requests, but I was hoping you could help me with a quick piece of data," versus "Sam, I need you to find some data." He tried those suggestions and made progress.

I know it may sound simple, but don't assume everyone thinks like you do or sees the obvious. They don't. And maybe you don't either.

—TODD

Listen carefully to the recipient's response and react appropriately. It's hard to predict how someone will respond to redirecting feedback, though the more you know about your people, the better you can anticipate their reactions.

Sometimes people justify or explain their side of the story. They'll offer excuses or their "whys." I'm fairly forgiving of the *why*, but unforgiving of the *what*. I know there are whys, lots of them, all the time. Some of them I can do something about; others not. The fact of the matter is we are where we are, so I might say next: "I didn't realize that was going on in your life. It sounds challenging. That doesn't change the fact that we've got to figure out how to get this done. Let's brainstorm how we could do that."

Don't be afraid of how emotions can manifest in physical ways during this conversation: flushed cheeks, automatic tears, contracted body language, sweating. Allow someone to react without feeling compelled to fix it immediately. Don't ascribe a judgment to it. If it interferes with delivering the feedback, give your employee a moment to collect themself.

CONSIDER THIS ⑦

The Key to Feedback

Although new leaders sometimes emphasize the problem, the most important part of delivering feedback is managing the emotional aspect. That's probably why a lot of leaders avoid these discussions altogether. Spend a significant amount of your preparation addressing the possible emotions of the discussion.

—TODD

Help your employee take responsibility for changing their behavior. You may find a team member unwilling to take responsibility for their behavior. Should that be the case, you might say something like, "Can you see that your actions are contributing to this problem?"

or "Do you agree that this behavior needs to change?" If the person avoids taking any responsibility, continue to present examples about the extent of the problem and its negative impact.

Codevelop an action plan. Your direct report has agreed that there's a problem and it's their responsibility to fix it—now what? Develop an action plan together. The person should understand what behavior you expect and find that expectation reasonable.

CONSIDER THIS ⑦

―――――

Reflect on Your Role

When you listen to a person's "why" after they receive redirecting feedback, consider what role you might have played, for better or worse. Have you delegated too much to them? Have you shifted priorities? Have you clarified exactly the outcome you're looking for? Does the person have the skills needed to get the job done?

If I'm part of creating the "why," I might also need to help address it. Then I can influence the "what."

You need to know when you can help and when to recommend further counsel. I might be a good coach, but I'm not a therapist. They may need outside counseling to deal with their more challenging "whys": past traumas, attention disorders, and pressing family problems.

—VICTORIA

In most cases, you'll get better results if the action plan comes from that person rather than from you. Try asking something like, "We've agreed on what needs to improve. What could you do differently to get there?" If they're unable to come up with a plan, give them more time or make suggestions.

The 6 Most Common Responses to Feedback

There are as many different types of responses to feedback as there are people. No one will have the exact same response as the next person, but we've seen these six categories present themselves most often.

1. The Excuse Maker

How this presents: This person acknowledges the problem but fails to take responsibility for it. "I know I avoid conflict, but that's just who I am," or "I don't share my opinions because the only person the team listens to is Jan."

Why it's happening: This person may struggle with admitting they need to improve, so they make themselves the victim by creating reasons for their behavior.

How to manage: If you hear this, consider what could be behind the person's fear of admitting a problem and making changes. Share areas in which you have been given feedback and help them see that all of us have areas we could improve. Also, while there are things they can't control, they can influence more than they think.

2. The Overreactor

How this presents: This person blows up and often verbally strikes back at the person giving feedback. Before you even finish your first sentence, they're telling you how wrong you are. "Why are you picking on me? I've given this company the last seven years of my life!" or "Well, that's your opinion."

Why it's happening: For whatever reason, this person can't comprehend being criticized or even coached. The feedback touches a nerve, so their emotions take over.

How to manage: Give them time to get their emotions in check to have a constructive conversation. "I appreciate your perspective on this and that you're angry. But as your manager, I'm paid to make a judgment call, and here's what must change . . ."

3. The Perfectionist

How this presents: This person feels so bad for "disappointing you" that you can see and feel their devastation; even the most minor feedback causes them great pain.

Why it's happening: The perfectionist does 99 percent of everything perfectly, so they truly don't need a lot of redirecting feedback. But when they do, it kills them because they thought they were doing everything right from the beginning. They want to be perfect every time. Not because of arrogance, but because they take such great pride in being one of your top performers.

How to manage: Use levity to warm them up a bit: "I want to give you some feedback. Because you are a superstar of superstars and you do everything so well, I notice that when there is something you might do a little better, it's hard for you to hear because you feel like you've disappointed me or others. Please know you haven't. So let's acknowledge that." Often these incredible employees start laughing and reply with something like, "Yeah, you're right. Tell me where I can improve."

4. The Poser

How this presents: This person will listen, usually agree with you—and then never change. They have the appearance of receiving feedback well—in fact they will often solicit it—but then go right back to what they were doing before.

Why it's happening: They're so ingrained in who they are that nothing changes. Posers are good people but usually only want reinforcing feedback. So they are continually seeking praise under the guise of asking for feedback, pretending to take in all of it but really only valuing the feedback that makes them feel good.

How to manage: Say something like, "Before I share this feedback with you, let me tell you what I've experienced. I know you want to improve and change, but remember when we talked about your tardiness and you said you would work on it? Nothing changed. So as we talk about this, could we take it one step further and discuss the behaviors we will actually see change? What goals do you want to set for yourself? How will we measure your progress?"

5. The Emoter

How this presents: Regardless of the type of feedback, this person gets very emotional, usually with tears.

Why it's happening: While it could be for any number of reasons, know that it can be a natural reaction.

How to manage: While it may sound obvious, be sure to have tissues on hand. Be aware and sensitive: "I know this is emotional, and I appreciate how you might be feeling. Do you need a moment, or would you like to continue this a little later?" Reiterate that your intent is to help them be successful.

6. The Mature Improver

How this presents: This person acknowledges the problem and takes responsibility for fixing it: "I know I'm risk-averse, and it's something I really want to improve."

Why it's happening: This person is a self-confident individual who understands we all have areas of improvement, and they see redirecting feedback as a chance to change—and sincerely appreciate it.

How to manage: Recognize this person's maturity and express appreciation for their willingness to take responsibility for their behavior.

—TODD

Summarize the discussion and thank the team member. Once you have both agreed to an action plan, recap what was agreed on, both verbally and in a follow-up email. "I'd like to briefly summarize what we talked about today. We both acknowledged that it's important for you to meet your deadlines, and we developed a plan to help you get there. Thank you for your effort. I think it will have a big impact on the performance of our team."

Provide support. Heading in the right direction is the key here, not overnight perfection. In the weeks that follow, don't overload your team member with additional behaviors they need to change; give them time to make adjustments. Provide reinforcing feedback every time they change their behavior. Your regular 1-on-1s are a great time to provide the support needed for sustainable change.

CONSIDER THIS ⑦

What happens if the behavior doesn't change?

If you notice that a person's behavior does not improve after your discussions and coming up with a plan of action, ask your employee how the plan is going and if there is anything you can do to help.

If you've addressed the issue multiple times with them, be extremely clear about the consequences if the behavior doesn't change, like a written warning, a lower score on a performance review, or even termination.

The discussion might sound like this: "I appreciate the efforts you've made in changing the behaviors we discussed. Unfortunately, we haven't seen the needed improvement. We're now going to a formal performance plan, which may result in you losing your position." While each organization has its own process for handling performance issues, your HR team should be involved and documentation is usually required.

—TODD

SKILL 3: SEEK FEEDBACK ABOUT YOURSELF

Sometimes when I put on cologne, I think I've applied a perfectly subtle amount—then my wife will say, "Are you kidding me? Go walk around outside for five minutes before I have an asthma attack."

There are physiological reasons why I can't smell my own cologne (our brains filter out familiar smells). It's the same thing with our job performance: we become numb to our own weaknesses, foibles, stumbling blocks, and habits. We need other people to point them out before we give someone an asthma attack.

I've smelled Scott's cologne, and I agree with his wife.

—TODD

While asking for feedback puts you in a vulnerable position, you have to learn to actually crave it. Make it your brand. Personally, I'm constantly asking for feedback, and believe that soliciting so much feedback has been responsible for whatever success I've had, as painful as it might have been to receive it at the time.

After my team went through a turbulent time, I decided to recalibrate through a focusing session that I usually led with clients. As a creative way to discuss the current status, I had everyone draw pictures of how they saw the team at the moment, illustrating our communication, execution, team spirit, collaboration, goal achievement, and more. The exercise puts people at ease; rather than sitting around discussing, you can be creative.

My team loved this idea and got right to work. To my horror, one team came back with a picture of a frantic, high-speed flight, with me as the captain wearing a turquoise scarf (that I apparently wore too often in real life), and the team members performing crazy duties in a chaotic environment. That picture will be forever instilled in my memory.

While I didn't feel great about this picture, I was proud of my team for being so candid. Now that our issues were out in the open, we could address them. I learned so much that day from them, and the picture was a meaningful and different way of getting feedback. It doesn't always have to be a 1-on-1 conversation in an office.

—VICTORIA

———

Over the years, I've gotten more deliberate about when and whom I ask for feedback. I have to carefully evaluate the feedback I get against my own priorities, capacity, and value system, and not just agree with the last person I talked to. As you're accepting feedback, develop a sense of context and accuracy: Did one person say that or seven?

Your team will be one of your most important sources of feedback. But they generally won't want to give it to you. They will be cautious because they've heard about—or experienced—managers lashing out, stunting people's careers, or just ignoring them. Your job is to make it safe for them to tell you the truth.

———

Now that you're in leadership, your title has become potentially threatening. It can create a barrier to feedback, so you'll need to make an extra effort to seek it out.

—TODD

———

There are so many good reasons to eagerly solicit feedback from your team:

- **It creates a thriving feedback culture.** The more you ask for feedback, the more your people become comfortable giving it, and also receiving it themselves.

- **It helps you grow personally.** Just as your team will grow from feedback, so will you. The practice will help you improve your skills, stay humble, and control your emotions.

- **It models for your team how to accept feedback.** It's never easy to hear what you're doing wrong, so do your best to show by example how to accept feedback graciously.

- **It helps your team feel heard and respected.** Feeling like they can come to you anytime with their concerns goes a long way to defusing resentment, rumors, and other forces that harm team cohesion.

6 STEPS TO GET GREAT FEEDBACK

Seek, and get, actionable feedback by using our six-part approach:

1. **Prepare people in advance and declare your intent.** Showing up in someone's office and asking for feedback will put them on the spot. Most people are going to say something like, "Oh, um, the meeting was great, boss!" Not helpful. Instead, let them know ahead of time that you'd like to get their feedback on, for example, how effective you are at conducting team meetings. Make it safe by telling them that you really want to improve in this area, and they can help. Then schedule a time *after* a team meeting or two when they've had a chance to think through what they want to share.

   If you haven't been in the habit of seeking feedback from your team, it will take some work to build trust. Be up front about why you're asking. Don't make your direct reports guess your motivations for requesting feedback.

   In terms of whom to ask for feedback, don't only pick your champions or your detractors. Get a cross section of people.

2. **Ask for specific feedback.** Generic questions like "How am I doing as a manager?" won't yield many insights. Provide more context and a specific area to work on. For example, I have asked people to observe me delivering a presentation and then email their comments to me. Some people tend to be more courageous in email than face-to-face, and it gives you some space to digest their comments.

   Use the words "advice" or "input" instead of "feedback." By choosing language that implies you're asking someone to share their expertise, you might avoid hitting the panic button, such as "I could use your advice on ways to better recognize our team's contributions" or "Can I get your input on my email communication and how I might improve it?"

Offer examples of feedback you've received in the past. This signals that you know you're not perfect and are open to feedback. For example, "Team members in the past have told me I can be unclear when I assign tasks. That was very helpful for me to hear, and it's something I'm working on. Any additional thoughts you might share with me?"

3. **Listen empathically.** Bring your Empathic Listening skills from Practice 2: Hold Regular 1-on-1s. Don't interrupt. Control your emotions, listen, and ask only clarifying questions. When receiving difficult feedback, you may feel devastated. Or you might feel like saying, "Are you kidding me? Do you have any idea how hard my job is?" Which is a great way to guarantee that you'll never get honest feedback again.

Forgive awkward deliveries. Many individual contributors haven't received training on how to give feedback in the workplace and have few opportunities to practice. As a result, their delivery might come across as too blunt, hesitant, or unpolished. Look past the delivery and focus on the substance of what they're saying and the intent behind it.

Go back to the "6 Most Common Responses to Feedback" in Skill 2 earlier in this section. Do you recognize yourself as one of them? Do you need to manage your own reaction accordingly?

4. **Acknowledge the feedback.** Once I've had time to digest the feedback and go through my stages of grief (anger, anger, anger, and denial), I meet with the person to debrief.

When I receive feedback, my first response is to bristle at it, probably like everyone else in the world. But you cannot lure people into your den and then be a snake. If you ask someone to share feedback at their own risk, you cannot punish them, hold it against them, or in any way make them regret it—primarily by becoming defensive. So you will want to say something like, "While your feedback was hard to hear, I really appreciate your willingness to share your observations with me."

Find the humility to be sincerely appreciative. Ask clarifying questions, but be careful not to frame questions as excuses ("So you don't think it's important to set high standards?" for example).

It probably wasn't easy for that person to share feedback, so show them some respect. You'll be more likely to get feedback from them in the future as well.

5. **Evaluate the feedback.** You have three options when a direct report or others share feedback: take it, don't take it, or do some additional investigating (i.e., ask your manager, peers, or other direct reports for feedback on the same behavior).

   This takes discernment. The feedback might not be helpful or relevant. (A colleague once got feedback that she was too short.) It might not even be about you. Once I was piloting an event and asked some colleagues to review it. At the end, one of my peers tore it apart, including sections everyone else was raving about. I started feeling insecure, but then I realized the feedback didn't seem to be about the event at all, but something—or someone—else. I thanked her, then chose not to act on that specific feedback.

6. **Commit to action.** Regardless of your decision, communicate your intentions to the person who gave you the feedback, either during the initial conversation or after you've thought it over. If you don't, you might as well say they were wrong to trust you. So consider saying, "I really appreciate our discussion and everything you shared. I'm going to think through what you and others have provided and then determine where I want to focus. Again, I found this so valuable, and I hope you will be willing to share your feedback in the future."

You won't give and accept feedback perfectly out of the gate, and that's okay. But learning to do it well is a distinctive feature of a great leader and manager—one your team deserves.

FEEDBACK:
ACTION PLAN

Answer these questions to prepare to give effective feedback—either reinforcing or redirecting.

PERSON OR PEOPLE WHO NEED THIS FEEDBACK:

DOCUMENT THE DETAILS

What is the issue I've noticed? *Example:* *• Rick talks over people in meetings.*	
What are the observable behaviors and facts around the issue? *Example:* *• He interrupted his colleagues in the past two meetings and took over my presentation.*	
What is the impact of this issue on results? *Example:* *• People have commented that they are unwilling to contribute because he takes up too much airtime. Meetings are our only chance to raise issues with the production team. Without everyone's input, we could face a product delay.*	

When and where will I share this feedback?

Example:

• *Our next 1-on-1.*

How I plan to open the conversation:

Examples:

• *"Rick, I'd like to share an observation about today's meeting. Do you have a few minutes?"*
• *"Rick, I noticed that . . . The impact is . . ."*

How do I expect the person or people to react? And how will I respond?

Example:

• *Rick is a perfectionist, so realize that he's doing most things extremely well.*

What are the main questions I want to ask?

Examples:

• *"Can you help me understand why this is happening?"*
• *"What might you do differently in the future and how can I help?"*

I will close the conversation by saying:

Examples:

• *"Thank you for your effort in this. It sounds like we agree that you'll do X and I'll do Y."*
• *"I'll send an email recapping what we've both agreed to, and then let's follow up on _____ [fill in date]."*

Take a moment to review this practice, and note the insights that most resonated with you.

_____

_____

_____

_____

_____

_____

_____

Jot down two to three action items you want to commit to.

_____

_____

_____

_____

_____

_____

_____

_____

LEAD YOUR TEAM THROUGH CHANGE

Most people think change is good—but only when it's their idea. When it comes from other people, it's not nearly as enjoyable. As MIT scientist and management expert Peter Senge said, "People don't resist change; they resist being changed."*

Great leaders must lead change, even when it originates from the corporate office, outside consultants, customer demands, economic turmoil, or competitors. And as a first-level leader, most of the change you face will be someone else's idea.

One of the leaders in our organization has a significant positive influence on his team and his own managers, in part because he not only executes change, he leads out on it. I'll call him Paul, because that's his name.

When Paul was a first-level leader, he was struggling to understand a new onboarding process the company had implemented—partly due to his lack of buy-in. He was concerned that the new process was making his team's life (and his) more difficult than necessary. He thought carefully about his concerns and how his role as a leader was to clear the path for this team and help them reach their goals. At the same time, he also wanted to help the organization achieve its larger goals.

---

* Senge, P. M. (2006). *The Fifth Discipline*. London: Random House Business.

He had the serendipitous opportunity to talk with our CEO at a sales conference where Paul respectfully shared his concerns in a private conversation. He simply said, "I want my team to know I'm completely supportive of the new onboarding process, but to be honest with you, I'm not. I'm sure I can get there with a better understanding of why we are doing it this way. Would you be willing to share with me how we decided on this process?"

After a transparent discussion, Paul not only had a much better understanding of the "why" behind the new process; he also knew how he could more effectively implement the change and even influence other leaders who had similar concerns.

Paul's action had a positive, lasting impression on our CEO, and it was one of the factors that led to the significant influence he has today, rising from first-level leader to senior executive.

If you're reading this and thinking, "So is Paul just good at managing up?" you don't know Paul. He, and other leaders like him, excel at being courageous and vulnerable in seeking to understand the "why" behind the "what." And one of the most effective ways a first-level leader can do that is to successfully lead out on change.

—TODD

To be clear, "leading out" doesn't mean coming up with change. In the above story about Paul, he didn't invent the onboarding strategy; he was asked to implement it. And even though he struggled with it at first, he had the courage, maturity, and humility to ask his leader to help him understand the change so he could authentically get on board.

Plenty of leaders can succeed during good times, but the true mettle of a leader emerges during times of uncertainty. When change comes your way (and it will), it is arguably one of the strongest tests of your leadership capability. Those leaders who show patience, stamina, emotional stability, resilience, and confidence are the most valuable to an organization and their team.

COMMON MINDSET	EFFECTIVE MINDSET
I control and contain change for my team.	I champion change with my team.

Entrepreneur and author Seth Godin writes, "In today's world, betting on chaos is the safest bet of all."[*] We're surrounded by change: layoffs, mergers, leadership shuffles, strategy switcharoos, and "helpful" software updates that often create more headaches than they fix. One of your most important responsibilities is keeping your team productive during upheaval. You can't just focus on the mechanics of change—processes, tasks, and training. You need to recognize and address the emotional aspect of change too. That's where change initiatives most often go off the rails.

Nothing will shape your team's ability to adapt to change more profoundly than the way *you* approach it. If you resist change or feel overwhelmed, confused, or skeptical, your team will adopt that same frame of mind.

THE FRANKLINCOVEY CHANGE MODEL

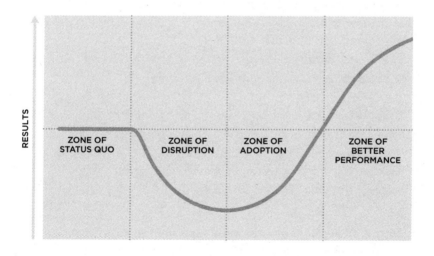

* Godin, S. (2012, July 30). Survival Is Not Enough. Retrieved from https://www .fastcompany.com/44216/survival-not-enough.

The outcomes of an organizationwide change are often unpredictable, as are most people's responses. The FranklinCovey Change Model is a tool to help all of us move through four common zones of adopting change.

One caveat: change management is the subject of intense study and many an organizational-development dissertation. This chapter is not one of those dissertations. We've intentionally created a simple, clear, and actionable model that will help leaders navigate the *emotional* aspect of change.

This model applies logic and predictability to what can otherwise seem like a chaotic process. It's a tool for diagnosing your team's responses to ongoing change—as well as your own—and helping everyone navigate the roughest parts to achieve acceptance and ownership.

Here's a helpful phrase to remember for the rest of this practice: "short and shallow." It's meant to remind you not to wallow or lose traction in any one zone. Instead, it will help you acknowledge each zone, spend the sufficient time necessary dealing with its challenges, and move forward. That will differ for every individual, team, and organization based on cultural tolerance for change, including your own. You're not trying to shortchange or eliminate any particular zone; instead you're trying to keep the time you spend in each zone as short and as shallow as reasonable. Sometimes just acknowledging the zone you're in is enough to move through it.

The model divides the complicated process of change into four zones, based on our natural emotional responses:

- **Zone 1: Status Quo.** You and your team are doing business as usual before the change occurs, and everyone is relatively comfortable. While change might seem desirable in some circumstances, that's probably because it's theoretical. But the theoretical quickly becomes real when change is actually imposed on you and your team.

- **Zone 2: Disruption.** Emotions run high and results suffer as everyone reacts to the news and its implications for them personally. It's a time of great stress and uncertainty. As information is shared and the process becomes somewhat clearer, you stop reacting and begin consciously developing a plan of action for your team and yourself.

- **Zone 3: Adoption.** Resistance and stress turn into acceptance, and for others, resignation (sometimes literally). You and your team identify ways you can adapt to the change and learn new ways of doing things. At the end of this zone, you may begin to see improved results. You may also find yourself squarely facing bad decisions or flawed strategy.

- **Zone 4: Better Performance.** The change initiative has largely been implemented and, ideally, you and your team are getting better results. But even if the change initiative fails (and many do) beyond your efforts, you and your team have likely increased your resilience and earned a brand of leading out when the next change comes your way.

Change is a sloppy process, but it can be better adopted with awareness of these four zones, especially if you can help make them short and shallow.

You can also use the model to diagnose where each team member is on the emotional curve at a given time. No two people respond to change in the same way or at the same rate. But when you can say, "Shawn is in Zone 3, but Megan is still stuck in Zone 2," you can address issues on an individual basis.

Great leaders help their team members reach Zone 4 as quickly and smoothly as possible. Preparing for change in Zone 1 and managing emotions in Zones 2 and 3 will help ensure that your team's change curve is short and shallow.

Finally, address your own journey through the zones as well. Don't discount your emotions, fears, and confusion. You may need to compartmentalize them briefly to keep your focus on the emotional well-being of your team, but don't let that temporary holding pattern manifest into permanent avoidance. Be comfortable legitimizing your concerns with your manager in private. If they haven't created a safe environment for you to do so, find someone else in a senior position whom you can disclose your concerns to. You deserve a safe haven to express your fears and uncertainties. Be mindful that you still need to convey an appropriate sense of confidence and momentum with your team. Balancing these two might feel incongruent, but it's a tension that every leader faces during change.

When I was working in a large corporation during the global financial crisis, our part of the organization needed to drastically cut costs. There were lots of rumors about layoffs, and people were understandably stressed.

I was leading a high-performing learning and development team, and they started to worry about who was going to be let go first. I brought them together and said, "Listen, I don't know what's going to happen. Yes, we might need to let someone go from our team. But just as we feel panicked, everyone in the organization is feeling the same way. That will create worse service for our clients, which will affect our results and, ultimately, our destiny. Let's talk about the bigger picture and what we're going to do about this. We need to continue to show the value our team brings to the organization." I also told them frankly, "I don't know when I'll have more information, and I don't know how much information I'll be able to share with you, but I'll do my best to be as transparent as possible."

I prepared myself to have to let go of some people on my team, and even be laid off myself. My husband and I discussed it and agreed that we needed a Plan B if my entire team (including me) was let go. That's something I recommend others do ever since that moment: When you are going through challenging times, create a Plan B. Then put it aside so you can focus on being present and executing Plan A.

Finally, we got the orders to cut a large number of managers on staff. We had a deadline of forty-eight hours to make our decision. I was assigned to a small task force making this happen. We knew we had to do this to save the company, but at the same time, we knew whomever we dismissed would be severely affected. We created the list, and then had to call in the managers one by one. It was an awful process I'll never forget.

When you have to be the bearer of bad news, it's so easy to make it about yourself and your feelings. In my case, I felt so sorry for the managers that I myself felt like crying. But you need to talk yourself out of that. Remind yourself: "This is not about me. What can I do to make this as humane an experience as possible for this person who knows exactly why they've been called to this meeting?"

Remember, this happened within forty-eight hours, while we still needed to run a business. Everyone was having different reactions: anger, shock, denial. We prepared all the managers who would be losing people on their teams with the Change Model and how they could deal with the reactions. We advised them, "Your team may be angry. They may cry or become emotional. And you need to be the bigger person in this. Let them have those reactions, including if they say mean things about you. That's okay, because it's not about you; it's about helping them go through what might be one of the worst experiences in their lives."

The shock and reactions might linger for longer than you think. In our case, it changed the paradigm that we were a golden, stable organization. Up to that point, people felt so safe. We had to work hard to get back the "winning team" feeling, even though our part of the organization had not performed badly from the start.

—VICTORIA

SKILL 1: PREPARE FOR CHANGE IN ZONE 1

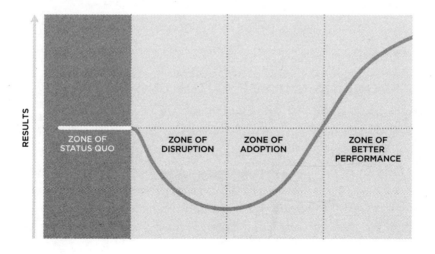

The Zone of Status Quo exists *before* change is introduced. You and your team are comfortable, and even if everything isn't ideal, you've developed workarounds. Things are predictable. Because of this, the longer the Zone of Status Quo lasts, the more likely your team will respond negatively when change arrives.

TRY IT OUT ⬡

Reflect on Your Tolerance for Change

Before you lead out on change, you have to master your own emotional response. Look at how you've reacted to change in the past. If your reaction was negative, ask why. Were you distrustful of management? afraid for your job? unhappy about not being consulted? resentful about the inconvenience? concerned or paranoid that your skillset wasn't adequate for the change?

Think of a current or an upcoming change you're facing. For a moment, put your personal agenda and needs aside. Reflect on the likelihood that this change is for the greater good of the organization. How could you better align to the change? Could the disruption even increase your relevance and influence?

—TODD

INTRODUCING CHANGE AT THE END OF ZONE 1

Being a champion of change begins when you recognize the unusual position you're in as a first-level leader. When change is handed down, you're expected to get behind it immediately and then implement it on the front lines. But too often, new managers assume that means they either have to carry the entire burden themselves, or limit the impact the change has on their team. Another mistake a new leader can make is thinking they get points with their team if they create an "us vs.

them" mentality, joining in with their team's criticism or backbiting about the change.

The best approach is to realize everyone needs to be exposed to the change as soon as possible. The more you insulate—and therefore isolate—your team from the new direction, the less secure and relevant they will be when the new strategy becomes permanent.

You're often the buffer between the leadership that's been planning the change and the people it ultimately affects. Not only do you have to process your own emotions about the change, but you also have to prepare for the trepidation of your team.

Communicating change simply, clearly, and with respect for the concerns and experience of your direct reports is key to kicking off a change initiative in a positive way. The following are some best practices for doing it right:

Preemptively address messaging with your boss and/or the appropriate stakeholders. Do you know why the change is being implemented, how it's going to be measured, or how long leaders expect it to take? You can't keep your people informed if you're uninformed. Be ready to go to your boss or other stakeholders and inquire in a curious, upbeat, and open-minded way, recognizing that they might not have all the answers and there will be some ambiguity that has to be understood. If everyone had all the answers, change initiatives would never fail. In fact, an astonishing 75 percent of change initiatives fail over the long term.[*]

Follow up on news of a company change with the whole team, preferably in person. Bring everyone together right away and explain what's happening so that everyone hears your interpretation of events at the same time and in the same way. This minimizes the chances of confusion, gossip, or anger about the order in which people were informed. Pay special attention to team members who work remotely—as always, include them via video rather than over the phone so you can better gauge their reactions, and they yours.

---

[*] Quarter of Employees Gain from Change Management Initiatives. (2013, August 29). Retrieved from https://www.towerswatson.com/en/Press/2013/08/Only-One -Quarter-of-Employers-Are-Sustaining-Gains-From-Change-Management.

When You're Not on Board with the Change . . . Yet

If you're still reacting negatively to the change when it's time for you to introduce it to your team, consider respectfully discussing your concerns with your boss (perhaps during your regular 1-on-1), like Paul did in my example.

Try saying, "Hey, can I book some time with you? I want to understand this initiative and how it affects my team. My goal is to understand it better so I can implement it better. I might share some frustrations and challenges. Please don't misinterpret them as me resisting the change." The vast majority of leaders will be open to this type of request, if handled properly.

-TODD

Be candid, comprehensive, clear, and fair. Even if the news has positive implications, most people associate change with something bad. Suspense or confusing language will only subconsciously magnify worry and dread. Be direct and clear. Keep your body language relaxed and your tone of voice calm. Avoid jargon and business speak.

If the change is seen as negative, don't bad-mouth those responsible for the change to make yourself look better in the eyes of your team. Respect people's intelligence and resilience by leveling with them about hard truths. If people have been let go, say so. If additional positions might be lost, acknowledge it. If this change is going to be difficult, admit it but follow up with details. Your people will cope with what's happening, but only if they can deal with the whole picture. Most people can handle bad news—they hate ambiguity or evasion.

I worked with a manager once who felt there always had to be an enemy in order for him to be the hero. He always made the organization the bad guy so that his team would see him battling in their favor. While their devotion and appreciation to him was clear, it really slowed things down when there wasn't an actual enemy to begin with. I think this might be more common than we think with leaders. This may provide a short-term high, but it's ultimately self-serving and not sustainable.

—TODD

Use "we" and "us," not "they" and "them." Resist the urge to blame organizational changes on management. To your team, you *are* "management." And even if you had zero input into what's happening, distancing yourself from it only fosters a sense of futility, as well as a potentially toxic "us against them" attitude. Aim for neutrality and openness in your announcement:

> Poor: "You guys aren't going to believe this, but we're merging with Competitor X. It's a decision made by management, and there isn't anything I can do about it."

> Better: "I learned some important news: We're merging with Competitor X. I know it's probably a shock—I'm still processing the news myself. Let me tell you what I know so far, and then I'd like to hear your questions and concerns."

Clarify how the change will affect your team. It's human nature for people to want to know how change is going to affect them: "Am I going to keep my job? Should I cancel my kids' summer camp? Should I call my spouse and tell them they can't retire next month?" Once while I was announcing an unfortunate set of layoffs, one of my team members interrupted me in the middle of my sentence to call his wife and tell her to cancel their driveway repavement. I don't share this to mock him; the opposite, in fact. Our careers are central to nearly every aspect of our lives, namely, supporting ourselves and our families. This impact isn't 100 percent under your control, but you can't minimize it. Tailor change messages for your team by letting them know how events are likely to impact their work, hours, compensation, relocations, and other factors. Be clear when future change is a certainty and when it's just a possibility.

Explain why the change is happening. The leaders who make decisions about a change initiative likely have had months to process the upheaval. Your frontline people don't have that luxury. From their perspective, change often comes out of nowhere. They have no runway to get used to the idea and deal with their feelings.

Just because the benefits of a change are self-evident to you doesn't mean they'll be obvious enough to your direct reports to overcome their natural resistance. Provide context—no one appreciates being told to change without knowing why.

If people don't have the real story about how the change came about, they'll start to make up their own version in their heads.

—VICTORIA

CONSIDER THIS (?)

What If *You* Are the Big Change?

Once when I took on the role of director, my promotion came as a major disruption to my peers, some of whom desperately wanted the role themselves. The change was quite difficult for the first six months. Fortunately, it wasn't my first leadership role, so I was able to manage the team through it with clear communication. But if it had been my first time as a manager, it might have killed my success.

When you're promoted to a leadership role, it might be a big change for the people around you. If my own boss and I had done the prework outlined here, we wouldn't have faced such an uphill start. Make sure your manager supports you; for example, by clearly communicating to your peers about changes ahead of time, or redirecting your former peers back to you if they continue to go above your head.

—VICTORIA

Acknowledge people's feelings. Encourage everyone to speak about their feelings honestly. Recognize that their feelings are legitimate, and let them know you are there to help them cope with their reactions as change progresses ("If you feel concerned about your ability to adapt to the new process, let's walk through it together during our next 1-on-1"). You'll defuse a lot of potential problems.

CONSIDER THIS ?

Announcing Positive Change

I once attended a great leadership course and learned a new system to track and execute our goals. I came back to my team with great enthusiasm. This new method was going to help everyone, right? I underestimated the extent to which I needed to explain the new initiative to my team. I was excited to jump in and positioned the change as a saving grace.

It's a classic trap when we're excited about a change. It took me a while to realize that my team wasn't as enthusiastic about it as I was. In their heads, this new system was something on top of what they already did, just more work for them.

I had to go back and redo the proper training with them. Then they said, "Now we get it!"

Interestingly, they never said to me that they hated it at the start. Only after they had bought in to the idea did they tell me how they had initially disliked the change.

When we're bracing for a change that we know people won't like, we know to be open, share the vision, get their buy-in, and help them through the adoption. But we often underestimate what it takes when we ourselves are enthusiastic about it. We still need to manage the process as properly as we would during a "difficult" change.

—VICTORIA

Those negative responses could include resentment, cynicism, anger at not being involved or consulted, or recruiting others to join their resistance. In most cases, open communication by the boss and an abundance of patience and empathy can eradicate all of these.

SKILL 2: MANAGE THE DISRUPTIONS IN ZONE 2

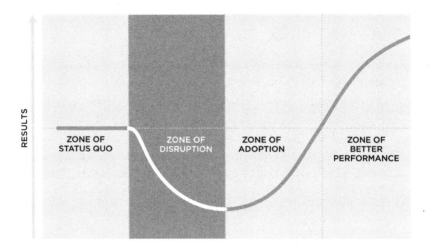

Once a change initiative is announced, you and your team move into the Zone of Disruption.

Wait, once it's *announced*, not implemented? That's right. Remember, the Change Model focuses not on activity but on the emotional responses to change, and those begin as soon as your team learns about change on the horizon.

This zone can be the toughest. All change creates disruption on some level—from lost time and increased costs, to intangibles like increased stress or damage to your culture. Even when employees feel positive about a change, factors like uncertainty and a steep learning curve can decrease productivity, increase downtime, and replace motivation with frustration. Any disruption affects the organization's results; the sloping line on the Change Model graph tells the story. The longer your team stays in the Zone of Disruption, the more your results suffer.

EVERYONE DESERVES A GREAT MANAGER

Your team members will stay in this zone until they:

- Understand what's changing and why.
- Understand what the change means for them personally (e.g., career, finances, schedule).
- Understand what they can do to regain some control over events.
- Decide on the actions they will take.

Team members who fulfill those four requirements have reached what we call the Point of Decision, when results start to rebound. You don't want anyone getting stuck in this zone, or they will redefine "normal" based on their reduced results. Your job is to minimize disruptions and help everyone find their way to the Point of Decision. These tools will help you achieve that. Remember, short and shallow.

One of your key assignments is to help change feel participatory for your team. How can they collaborate to influence the change? Make yourself and the team part of something exciting and transformative, when possible. We recognize that not all change lends itself to enthusiastic embrace, but the more you can involve your people in the process, the better.

As effective as your first communication might have been, your team will need time to process and understand the change. They will talk about it, worry about possible repercussions, and have new questions. This is natural. Resist trying to control negative reactions that make you uncomfortable. Give your team some elasticity to deal with their emotional responses. Remember, your role is to clarify, explain, resist spinning, and keep them updated.

If intense emotions are present, your people may forget much of the detail you shared. They may also find their ability to adapt compromised by anxiety or the desire to resist change. One solution is to communicate comprehensively and constantly. Be transparent. Tell people what's happening and why, as it happens. Listen to their questions and find answers as quickly as possible. Information and action are the antidotes to fear.

Check in with each team member frequently. By touching base with each person individually, you can ask open-ended questions that will help you better understand their state of mind and, if appropriate, suggest ways you can help. If you already do weekly 1-on-1s (see Practice 2), this process should be much easier.

Examples of questions you might ask:

- "How are you feeling about yesterday's news?"
- "What concerns do you have at this point that haven't been addressed?"
- "Have you been through something like this before in your career? What were some of the things you learned during that process?"
- "What can I do to make things easier?"

Minimize anxiety and quell rumors with information: "I can understand why you're concerned—doubling the team's size over the next year will present plenty of challenges. But the managers I've spoken with have assured me that if we need more space, we'll remain in the city, at least for the foreseeable future."

Express solidarity: "I agree it will be a tough transition—we'll all need to help each other through it."

Don't panic if someone asks a question or makes a comment that catches you off guard: "Thanks for bringing that up. I'll need some time to look into it and will share what I learn with the whole team tomorrow." And then do it.

Walk your talk. Teams always watch their managers closely, but your behavior will be scrutinized even more during times of change, simply because people may be trying to figure out what the change really means and how to respond. They will take your actions, reactions, emotions, and attitudes as cues for what the team's culture is now and how they should respond to what's happening.

Be mindful of what you say, how you say it, and how you react to change-related news that may be less than ideal. The calmer and more confident you are, the more your direct reports will focus on how they can adapt to the change too.

Address cynicism. No leadership team implements change because they're bored. Change is necessary because of the adage "change or die." Innovation and growth require new ideas, processes, and paradigms. Regardless of the industry, the global pressures of competition and shareholder growth mandate change, and everyone hopes it's the right decision.

One of the problems with change is that most people initially believe a change will make things worse rather than better. Some view new initiatives as the "change du jour," riding out the initiative because they're confident it will fail and the status quo will resume. The better bet is to get on board, lead out, and engage your team early so that all of you are set up for success on the other side.

Here's a helpful paradigm. In their book *How Will You Measure Your Life?*, Clayton Christensen, James Allworth, and Karen Dillon discuss two different types of strategy: deliberate and emergent. Deliberate strategies begin and end intact. But according to the authors, close to 93 percent of successful strategic initiatives change along the way. In some cases, the end strategy looks nothing like the initial plan. These are *emergent* strategies.*

As a first-level leader, you will find it helpful to understand ahead of time that a change will usually look different eighteen months later. Knowing this helps us be more forgiving, more tolerant, and more nimble throughout the process. You can become more adaptive and move through the zones of change faster if you don't get wrapped up in the fact that the strategy may emerge over time.

Rather than ignore skepticism, lean into it. It's okay to feel skeptical about change, and it's healthy to let your team air their concerns. But don't let the conversation turn into a festival of cynicism or finger-pointing. Draw on the empathy you learned in Practice 2. Simply feeling heard and having concerns recognized is an important part of coping. Giving your people that opportunity can make a big difference.

No announced change can have been thought through with every consequence—positive or negative—ticked and tied. Leaders are people

---

* Christensen, C. M., Allworth, J., & Dillon, K. (2012). *How Will You Measure Your Life?* New York: Harper Business.

too. Most change initiatives evolve. Recognize there are likely hundreds of data points and variables under scrutiny, and have some faith in your leadership. Assume good intent. There might be more to the picture than you currently understand, and seek out answers to your larger questions to help you and others get on board. The more you adopt this mindset, the less anxiety you'll have.

Confront chronic resistance and regression. Some people will continue to resist change, even after their colleagues are on board. Others might look like they're adapting to change but then regress to old behavior. Deal with such resistance head on, but with finesse and restraint, because such opposition isn't always a matter of stubbornness. If you trample someone's concerns, you may never get to the true cause of their noncompliance. As suggested before, patience, empathy, and perhaps a healthy dose of listening to their concerns will pay dividends. If it doesn't, you may need to exercise some straight talk and clarify that the train has left the station—you'd like them to be on it, but if they can't find their seat, they may need to pick a different destination.

Is the resistance a phase, a statement, or a deep, intractable mindset? Is the person a concerned employee with valid challenges, or an unreasonable agitator? Is the person engaged and high-performing? (It's surprisingly common for people who have thrived in an old environment to resist change because they have the most to lose from it.) Is the resistance overt or covert? Hidden resistance might indicate that you haven't created a team culture that encourages open dialogue and transparency. Your job is to model that it's safe to tell the truth throughout your career so that culture is in place when needed.

The aim of all these tips is to reach the Point of Decision, where the majority of your team buys in to the change and is ready to move into Zone 3.

During the crisis with the layoffs I shared earlier in this chapter, we had to help the team continue working while dealing with the emotional impact of layoffs. The preparation I mentioned in Zone 1 helped tremendously. It was important to share as much information as I could.

I had to help the team see the bigger picture—in this case, a possible disruption of the entire organization—and how they could play an active role. The team and I discussed how important it was to go out to other departments and support people there, rather than hide in our offices.

—VICTORIA

SKILL 3: ADAPT QUICKLY TO CHANGE IN ZONE 3

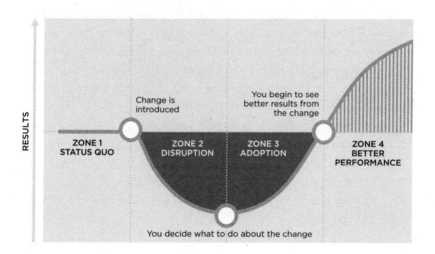

Change is hard, and it doesn't always end in a beautiful upward arc of success for everyone. Change can mean having to let people go, or result in people who don't want to get on board ultimately choosing to leave. Once change takes hold and begins to drive behavior, that's when it's most likely to fail.

In this zone, you and your team have made it past the Point of Decision and begun to adapt to the change's new rules. This is where stuff gets real. When you begin this zone, you're in a results abyss. Your people have spent all their time adapting to new rules, technologies, procedures, culture—essentially reinventing how they work. And now your job is to help them pivot from learning back to execution in this new reality.

Turning the "results" curve upward means more work, so it's important to evaluate everything you and your team members are doing and decide what makes sense to start, continue, or stop. The quicker you can adapt to the change, the faster everyone will feel good about the sacrifices you've made and see the benefits. Short and shallow!

In a perfect world, the curve in the Zone of Adoption looks like this:

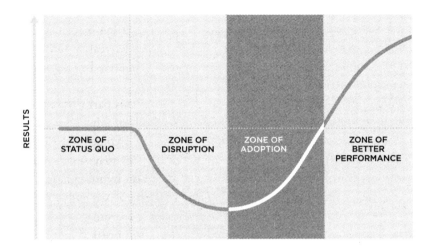

However, in the real world, the curve looks more like this:

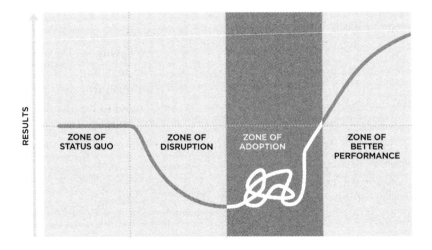

At this stage, your team is starting to use a new software dashboard to manage sales, learning to work with new vendors, managing an increased workload that their departed colleagues formerly owned, finding the bathrooms in new offices, or dealing with whatever change was handed down to you from on high as you try to get back to business. This does not happen smoothly, but in fits and starts. Newly installed back-end systems and hardware go down, frustrating everyone. Last-minute changes are made but unintentionally not communicated to the people on the front line—you and your team. Some of your team members' attitudes and compliance might regress as reality sinks in: what was ineffective but instinctive is now more effective but demands a lot more effort.

That's normal, but it doesn't mean it's easy. As this part of the process begins, you should shape people's expectations of what's to come. For example, if you're dealing with a technology change, you might say, "For the next few weeks or months, some of us may not be able to work on autopilot like we earned the right to do by mastering our old processes. We all might feel slower and clumsier as we continue to navigate new procedures and inadvertently revert to some of our old habits. Technology, process, and communication will break down from time to time. But it's temporary."

The tools here will help you keep that promise:

Reset and reprioritize expectations at both the team and individual levels. See Practice 3: Set Up Your Team to Get Results.

Focus on what matters (and say no to the rest). To make the uphill climb through the Zone of Adoption, focus on activities that support that effort and say no to those that don't. Saying no isn't easy, but if you take on too much at this vital stage, you may never find the momentum to pull through this zone. Shield your team from anything unrelated to mastering the new behaviors they'll need to be successful.

Use a scoreboard to track progress. Refer to Practice 3: Set Up Your Team to Get Results for more information on using scoreboards. Consider creating one specifically for the change process.

Create and celebrate early wins. As you move through the Zone of Adoption, your team members will need to see regular signs of progress if the change is going to remain urgent, or remain at all.

Consider what short-term wins you could steer your team toward to help them feel a sense of progress and momentum. A short-term win is a meaningful improvement that's obvious to everyone and unambiguously related to the change you've all been working on. Tangible costs savings due to the new process? *That's a win.* A happy customer? *Win, win.* Finally solving a technical problem with the calendaring software that's been driving your team crazy for two years? *Win, win, win.*

Remember that bringing your team through change is largely about managing emotions. Keeping team morale high will help support the effort it takes to get out of this zone.

Learn from mistakes. Change requires trying new things, and when people attempt something out of their comfort zone, they're bound to make mistakes. It's entirely possible to maintain a high bar for performance while remaining encouraging and upbeat. A smile, a compassionate tone of voice, and an acknowledgment of the person's effort can go a long way: "Thanks for trying the new consultative approach we talked about in that call. I really appreciate your willingness to give it a shot. May I give you some advice for next time? Let me share something I learned in my own attempt."

When we were trying to make the switch from one email system to another, one of our people called me on a Sunday and said, "I can't see any of my appointments on my phone." I said, "We sent out an email that showed you how to do that," but as the words were leaving my mouth, I knew we'd messed up. She said, "Todd, I got four hundred emails last week, and while I'm sure it's in there somewhere, I've got a client call in two hours and I can't get on it."

I learned that real life takes precedence over the best-laid plans. By asking better questions and involving people sooner, I could have anticipated potential issues and been out in front of them.

—TODD

Mistakes are part of any change initiative. Once you truly believe this, your team will come to believe it. Your thoughts, words, and actions must be congruent to create an environment where mistakes become safe learning opportunities. You may need to further coach team members on skills related to the change, which entails more than signing someone up for a training course. Use your 1-on-1s to set learning goals together and explore ways to get there. You can pair team members with mentors to give them additional perspective and a channel for feedback.

Have regular, open conversations about the change and its effects with your team as a group and/or in 1-on-1s. This is so important, we're going to reinforce it again. If you lock yourself in your office until the climate improves, your team won't forget it—or forgive you. Instead, rise to the challenge, which isn't a one-time event. Listen to and support your team members, and in the process, build trust and validate any ongoing confusion.

Give your team the outlet they need to voice their concerns: "It's been a crazy week here. I wanted to touch base and hear from you about how you're feeling. What concerns and questions do you have?"

Because everyone processes change differently and at their own pace, it's also a good idea to follow up with people in their 1-on-1s. That way you can ask open-ended questions to better understand each person's state of mind, reframe the change in ways that tap into their motivations and goals and, if appropriate, suggest ways you can help. Remember, you can't communicate enough during a change. Frequent and transparent communication is key.

Don't "spin" or downplay the difficulty of the situation. If you've ever been told immediately after getting bad news that it's "actually a great opportunity," you know how insulting and demoralizing it is to be fed a line. Instead of raising the team's spirits, such talk will make them angry and rebellious. Respect your team enough to be truthful and realistic about where everyone is in the process in ways that don't inhibit momentum. Your job isn't just to be a repository of complaints and concerns; you also have to *lead* your team and maintain momentum to earn the respect that comes from triumph.

Recruit "change evangelists" from your team to keep people moving. Within your team, you will probably have people who adapt to change more easily and regard it with more enthusiasm. Make allies of them. Recruit them to help the more change-resistant team members or people who are struggling with a new process or technology. Don't play favorites (as that can have the opposite effect in morale than you want), but encourage your evangelists to lend a hand, lend an ear, and bring positive energy around the change to the office every day.

During an enormous technological change at our organization, one of the initiative's leading champions became one of its greatest opponents once she saw what it meant for her department. But by helping her get clarity on the tangible benefits of the switch, the leadership team turned her back into a key cheerleader for the effort. Her enthusiasm became an essential support for morale.

Listen compassionately when people vent, but don't join in. There's a big difference between showing that you care and airing your own grievances when employees vent. Listen, ask questions, and acknowledge team members' feelings, but stop there. As tempting as it may be to join in complaint sessions, doing so could damage your credibility and make your team feel even worse. Make it about them, not you.

Ask your leader for feedback and help. They might have a different perspective on why the change isn't working and may be able to help you turn things around. In some organizational cultures, asking for help is thought to mean "I'm incapable." But asking for help is a sign of confidence, teachability, and the drive to get it right.

SKILL 4: SEEK FEEDBACK AND CELEBRATE SUCCESS IN ZONE 4

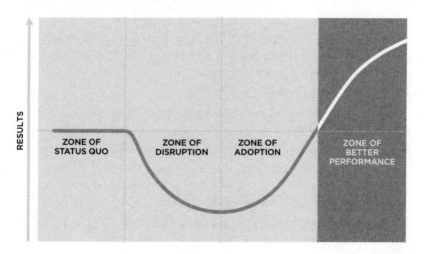

When you finally reach the Zone of Better Performance, you begin to see real benefits from the change that you've struggled through. You take control of the change and use it to your advantage. Here, the results you get begin to look better than when you first started out.

Even your most reluctant direct reports finally get on board. People who were relentlessly negative become more positive—sometimes because they have no choice. The benefits that were self-evident to management become self-evident to everybody. Now wins become more frequent and tangible results more apparent. This is definitely the time to celebrate and reward everyone involved in making this transformation a success. But it's also the time to avoid complacency. The lessons from achieving your goals—and even from failing—can pave the way for future success and better performance.

What did you learn about your employees' capacity and personalities that you could leverage outside the context of the Change Model? Are there individuals with leadership or communication skills you (and possibly they) were unaware of? Has openness about anxiety or emotions fostered a new sense of camaraderie and closeness among your team that you can take into future endeavors? Did you improvise processes or solutions that were met with unexpected success?

Chart key learnings about what worked and what didn't during the change initiative; do it with your team if you can. Then speculate: How could any or all of it be applied to increasing performance even more?

Seek feedback on how to better lead change. Review Practice 4: Create a Culture of Feedback for ideas on how to do this.

Make new goals, if needed. Revisit Practice 3: Set Up Your Team to Get Results if you need to formulate new goals for the team or individuals as a result of the change.

Build team capability for future changes. More change is coming, sooner or later. What can you and your team take away from this change initiative that will make future change easier and future journeys through the zones faster?

- What mistakes could have been prevented?
- What best practices should be preserved for future changes?
- What type of resistance did you encounter and why?
- How could you more effectively manage your team's emotions in the future?
- If you were to create a change "operations manual" for your team, what would be included?
- Assess your degree of "short and shallow"—is there anything you can learn from the duration spent in each zone?

Get into the habit of asking, "What could we be doing better?" and then following through on the best ideas. Actively build a healthy team culture in which feedback is constant and framed constructively, ensuring your people are ready to be communicative and transparent when changes hit. Start using 1-on-1s with your direct reports as a tool to explore learning and development goals so that your team's skillset keeps pace with your industry.

During times of change, your role is to lead your people through so they can adapt quickly and come out the other end with better performance. By demonstrating that you can thrive during uncertainty, you'll likely accelerate your own leadership trajectory as well.

REFLECTION GUIDE:
ADAPTING TO CHANGE

Change often happens so fast that you may not pause to assess the situation in a balanced way. But when you do, you'll be better equipped to adapt to the change—and help others do the same. Jot down your answers to the prompts below. And give this guide to your direct reports so they can reflect on their own responses.

DATE: **COMPANY CHANGE:**

Which zone am I in for this change? Which zones are my team members in?

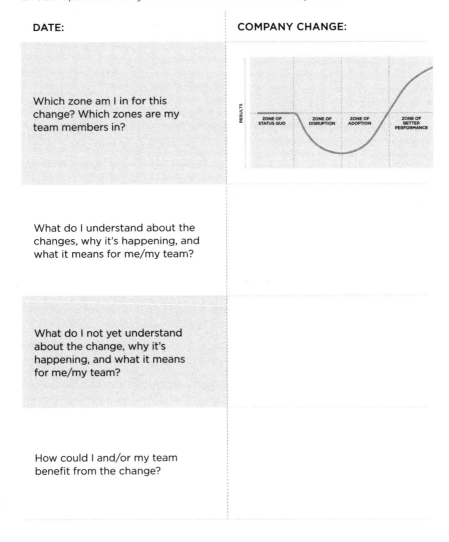

What do I understand about the changes, why it's happening, and what it means for me/my team?

What do I not yet understand about the change, why it's happening, and what it means for me/my team?

How could I and/or my team benefit from the change?

EVERYONE DESERVES A GREAT MANAGER

What are the obstacles, thoughts, or feelings that could keep me/my team from embracing the change?

What makes the most sense to start, continue, or stop in order to adapt to the change?

What are ways we can measure or hold ourselves accountable to know whether the change is successful?

What are one to three actions I can take to help myself and/or my team adapt to the change?

PLANNER:
COMMUNICATE A CHANGE TO YOUR TEAM

How you explain and talk about a company change is the first critical step toward helping your team understand and embrace the new way. Use this guide to formulate an effective message.

DATE:	COMPANY CHANGE:

HOW WILL THE CHANGE AFFECT MY TEAM?

What is the organization's message about this change?	
What are one to three ways that this change could be challenging for my team?	
What are one to three ways that this change could benefit my team?	
Given what I know about my team members, how do I expect them to react to this news?	

EVERYONE DESERVES A GREAT MANAGER

HOW WILL I COMMUNICATE THE CHANGE?

I will start the meeting by being as clear, direct, and detailed as I can be, saying:

I plan to use this language to explain why the change is happening:

I plan to use this language to explain what this news means for our team:

The truths I want to acknowledge (without bad-mouthing anyone) are:

Questions I will ask to encourage the team's honest feedback:

HOW WILL I COMMUNICATE THE CHANGE?

Phrases I can use if I'm asked a
question I can't answer:

I will close the meeting by sharing
next steps and how I will continue
to communicate:

HOW WILL I FOLLOW UP AFTER I COMMUNICATE THE CHANGE?

Questions I plan to ask team
members in follow-up
1-on-1 meetings:

Messages I want to continue to
reinforce with my direct reports:

Take a moment to review this practice, and note the insights that most resonated with you.

_____

_____

_____

_____

_____

_____

_____

Jot down two to three action items you want to commit to.

_____

_____

_____

_____

_____

_____

_____

_____

MANAGE YOUR TIME AND ENERGY

A Note from Scott

When it comes to this practice . . . Reader, I have sinned. For too long, I didn't value personal time—my team's or my own. It wasn't until fairly recently that I realized how important it is to manage my time and energy, and empower my team to do the same.

Fortunately, Victoria has long been an expert on this practice and is helping me transform personally. She exemplifies time and energy management as a leader, coaches her team to implement best practices, and keeps up with her own wellness practice as a credentialed yoga instructor and running coach. Victoria will take the mic in the following pages.

COMMON MINDSET	EFFECTIVE MINDSET
I am too busy to take time for myself.	I must manage my time and energy to be an effective leader.

My family is lucky to own a country house in Sweden, where we can come together and invite friends from near and far. The oldest building on the property dates back to the fifteenth century. The land is situated in the midst of the Swedish woods, next to a small lake with lots and lots of green lawns surrounding the houses. Even though guests are wowed by the nature, the midnight sun, and the old farm, the biggest attraction is always the robot lawn mowers.

My father is an early adopter of new technology, and we were among the first to get these lawn-mower robots. The robots spend their days working across the lawns, cutting the grass, while we "the people" busy ourselves with more creative and rejuvenating social activities. Someday we will tell our grandchildren about a time when we actually spent part of our summer holidays mowing the lawns, because they will never have seen someone doing it manually.

By then, lawn mowing won't be the only "profession" that will have ceased to exist. Most if not all jobs of today that are routine and repetitive will be replaced by artificial intelligence. In the future, our success will depend on our ability to use our whole brain and human skills of creativity, strategy, emotional intelligence, critical thinking, and vision.

To feed your brain, you need to manage your time and energy, and for long-term results, you must coach your team to do the same—especially because we're now working more than ever, burning out more than before. Gallup reports that about two-thirds of the workforce is now struggling with professional burnout.* I'm afraid I too have fallen into the trap of ignoring my own energy needs, and it was a lesson I haven't forgotten.

When I interviewed for a high-pressure job to turn around a department, I made it very clear that they would be hiring a parent of young children. I emphasized how I would need to be home for dinner every night. They were completely supportive and offered me the job. I was excited to dive in and had ambitions of achieving success within six months.

---

* Gallup, Inc. (n.d.). Employee Burnout, Part 1: The 5 Main Causes. Retrieved from https://www.gallup.com/workplace/237059/employee-burnout-part-main-causes.aspx.

With this goal in mind, I arrived at work at 7:00 a.m. each day in order to be home in time for dinner. Then 6:30 a.m. And earlier and earlier, until one day I glanced at the clock as I logged in and realized it was 5:23 in the morning.

Nobody was telling me, "Victoria, you need to work thirteen hours a day." But I was ambitious and determined to reach my goal. I thought that this was the right way to get there.

About six months into the job, I started feeling a sharp pain in my eye. Finally, after both my team and family pushed me, I went to the doctor, who said, "No wonder you're in pain; you have pink eye, a sinus infection, an ear infection, and a fever." I remember crawling into bed and resting for the first time in six months. I was so exhausted that I thought, "Ahhh, this feels great." Even with pink eye!

Not only was I suffering physically, I was far from my goal of turning the department around. I was pressuring myself to get results quickly, but my strategy of never resting worked against me.

My behavior had to change—to start, I couldn't get up at 4 a.m. anymore. But what really needed to change was, of course, my paradigm. Neglecting my health was certainly not leading to better, faster results. I decided I would work smarter, not harder, and do my best during a reasonable workday to allow myself time with my family. If that wasn't enough, maybe this role wasn't right for me.

I'm not suggesting that we're all in a position to leave jobs that drain us, but we can probably control some aspects of our roles that affect our time and energy. Stay focused on those levers, and you'll find that your influence expands. And the truth is that if I had continued burning myself out, I wouldn't have had that job at all.

I still worked hard, but I carefully deemphasized other less important roles. Eventually, I got the results I was aiming for—maybe not in six months, but over time—and more importantly, with my health and relationships intact.

Many, many people struggle with this challenge, including your own employees most likely. While the cultural norms are slowly catching up to the science, you might have to lead out on this in your organization. More often than not, a Paradigm Shift is needed. You probably already know what you need to do in order to build and maintain energy for yourself, but knowing and doing are often very different.

As you progress on your leadership track, you must decide how you're going to work, balance your life, and renew yourself. Establish the patterns now that will serve you long term. Resist the natural temptation to neglect your health, professional development, or personal life. Identify your needs. Model this for your team.

We've packed this chapter with practical suggestions, but more than any other practice, what works in this area will vary across individuals, companies, cultures, and countries. We'll begin with managing your energy, move on to managing your time, and end with helping your team do the same. As you figure out what works for you, remember that your priorities, needs, and methods will not be the same as your team's. Balance the best practices and principles we discuss with the real world. Do what works for you.

SKILL 1: MANAGE YOUR ENERGY

A few years ago, I was going through old books in the attic and found my grandmother's copy of how to keep a successful home, a book written in the 1950s. I was thrilled and expected to laugh out loud at all the old-fashioned statements. When I reached the section on health, I braced myself. But to my surprise, the advice in the book could have been written today. In short, it recommended moving every day, ideally doing some morning "gymnastics," and limiting sugar and wheat in your diet.

Similarly, during my studies to become a yoga instructor, I learned about the Vedas, sacred Sanskrit texts written thousands of years ago. I kept exclaiming (much to the annoyance of my fellow students), "Wow, this is exactly what we teach in our leadership solutions!" Theories I thought were fresh and new had been around a long time. The difference now is that we have the brain science to support them.

Most of us can easily recite all the things we need to do to manage our energy: sleep seven to eight hours, eat leafy greens, and exercise. Our shelves are full of books on the topics, with podcasts and blogs talking about it day after day, and new research studies continuously proving the need to manage our energy. So if we all "know" that energy contributes to performance, why is the rate of burnout higher than ever in today's workforce?

Over the years, I have worked with so many leaders struggling with work-life balance. A spectrum of causes exist. Some people deprioritize their own health out of a sense of nobility, putting their own needs last in order to be a great leader. Others ignore everything else because they're so passionate about their job or fearful they'll fall victim to the next round of cuts. Whatever the reason, a few best practices can help you better meet your energy needs. On the following pages, we want to share some tools and ideas you can use like an à la carte menu: pick what will help you manage your energy in the best way.

Review your own body clock throughout your day. Recall Daniel Pink's ideas of energy peaks, troughs, and recoveries in his book *When*, which we discussed in Practice 2. Begin by simply noticing your energy and what affects it. Starting today, be mindful of the particular parts of your day where your energy is naturally high and low, and notice if there's a consistent pattern over the next week or two. If so, you might become more aware of how you can capitalize on your peaks and minimize your troughs.

Remember Scott's rundown of his day in Practice 2 and his realization that his optimal time for 1-on-1s was in the morning? Similarly, analyze which of your team members are matched or mismatched with your own energy variations. You might find some insights—whoever has their 1-on-1 at 9 a.m. might be getting a better meeting than the team member you meet with at 3 p.m. Do you need to switch it up or better match others' peaks and troughs?

When you went into a 1-on-1 or another focused meeting, how did the time of day impact your contribution to that meeting? Which days were you full of energy and when did you struggle? How did your energy vary in different settings—at work or at home?

Once you start to notice any highs and lows in your energy levels, ask yourself why. What happened just before? What didn't happen? How did your environment, eating, or physical movement affect your energy level? Are you making a conscious decision to leave the previous meeting and its emotional impact behind?

Think about your job. What tasks or events give you the most energy? What are the things that bring you joy? Out of all your job responsibilities, which ones drain your energy? When do you have a great time at work? When did you last have a good laugh?

Consider these ups and downs. What activities should you schedule during your peak hours? What would be possible if you restructured your day or week? To get the most out of an important assignment, should you do it at a different time? Are there things you dread and tend to procrastinate? What can you do to make them bearable . . . or even pleasant?

I try to consider these questions when scheduling my 1-on-1 meetings, and when I block off time for thinking, producing, and tackling dull administrative tasks. Before going into an assignment that requires my full focus, I will often take a quick, brisk walk to get some fresh air and clear my head.

We all have our own body clock and different levels of energy, focus, and creativity throughout our days. We can use the weekly and daily planning in Skill 2 to our advantage here. Maybe you can't optimize the timing of every meeting and task—many leaders are desperate to simply fit all their responsibilities into a packed calendar—so think of it more as a long-term plan.

THE 5 ENERGY DRIVERS

When it comes to energy, most of us would welcome more of it. So let's review the 5 Energy Drivers, originally explored in our bestselling book and solution *The 5 Choices: The Path to Extraordinary Productivity.* These five drivers affect your energy levels:

- Sleep
- Relax
- Connect
- Move
- Eat

Take a moment to assess yourself on each of these drivers. Give yourself a benchmark against which to measure your progress as you enact the strategies in this practice. Note that if you're down in one driver, it tends to affect the others. You can do this assessment regularly—it's not a static test you take once. We recommend you review it every six months.

ASSESSMENT:
DO A PERSONAL ENERGY AUDIT

How are you doing with managing your prime sources of energy? Rate yourself in the following areas, with **0** as "never" and **10** as "always." Where you come up short, commit to improve.

SCORE PER AREA: 0–6=PROBLEM AREA   7–15=AVERAGE   16–20=DOING GREAT

SLEEP

I sleep the same amount each night (and don't use weekends to catch up on sleep).

1   2   3   4   5   6   7   8   9   10

I get good-quality sleep each night.

1   2   3   4   5   6   7   8   9   10

One change I will make to improve:

_____ TOTAL

RELAX

I have effective coping strategies to deal with stress.

1   2   3   4   5   6   7   8   9   10

My lifestyle supports my ability to manage stress.

1   2   3   4   5   6   7   8   9   10

One change I will make to improve:

_____ TOTAL

CONNECT

I connect regularly with important people in my life.

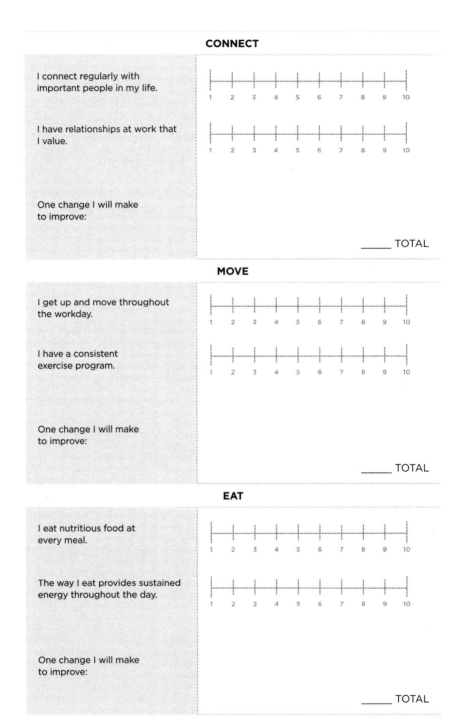

1 2 3 4 5 6 7 8 9 10

I have relationships at work that I value.

1 2 3 4 5 6 7 8 9 10

One change I will make to improve:

_____ TOTAL

MOVE

I get up and move throughout the workday.

1 2 3 4 5 6 7 8 9 10

I have a consistent exercise program.

1 2 3 4 5 6 7 8 9 10

One change I will make to improve:

_____ TOTAL

EAT

I eat nutritious food at every meal.

1 2 3 4 5 6 7 8 9 10

The way I eat provides sustained energy throughout the day.

1 2 3 4 5 6 7 8 9 10

One change I will make to improve:

_____ TOTAL

Assess your low scores—are there any immediate action items you could do to boost one of the drivers? It's possible you could integrate some lifestyle changes *tonight* that could pay big dividends in the hours and days to come.

Low scores represent an opportunity to increase your energy. Here's our best advice to improve each driver.

Sleep

- **Understand how vital sleep is to your overall health, specifically your brain health.** The renowned neuroscientist Dr. Daniel Amen likens sleep to "washing your brain" each night.* Seven hours of sleep is the standard; don't be shamed into believing the myth that four hours of sleep is sustainable.

- **Create space between your active, full-on day and your bedtime. Find a routine that works for you.** Personally, I turn off my phone and leave it out of reach from my bed. (I don't have enough impulse control to have it within reach.) I prepare a cup of herbal tea and write a few lines in my journal, summarizing the day. Finally, I read if it's not too late. I try to avoid reading business books that make me think about all the things I want to focus on the following day. Instead, I read fiction. A note of warning here: If the book is too good, it works against me, because I can't put it down!

- **Relaxing activities and routines, such as evening yoga and meditation, can also aid sleep.** I try to avoid a late-evening run or workout, as that keeps me up longer. Identify what type of activities calm you.

- **If it works for you, try a "go to sleep" app.** But watch out for the temptation to use your phone to check messages.

- **Your own best advice to yourself:**

_____

_____

---

* Rescue Your Brain Health [Interview by S. Miller]. (2018, July). Retrieved from https://resources.franklincovey.com/home/on-leadership-with-scott-miller-episode -08-dr-daniel-amen.

Relax

- **Don't confuse relaxation with numbness.** If your idea of fun is primarily TV binges, gaming marathons, or long naps, your relaxation might be draining rather than renewing you. Note how you feel afterward. Do you truly feel better? If not, try swapping those "relaxing" activities for a hobby that actually increases your energy.

Recently after an exhausting week, I parked myself on the couch for a relaxing Friday night with a movie and a huge barrel of Hi-Chew candies. The next morning, I woke up in the same spot, surrounded by (and this is not an exaggeration for dramatic effect) more than one hundred Hi-Chew wrappers. I felt more tired than ever.

Are any of your go-to relaxation methods actually exhausting? Could you replace them with something creative, active, or social?

—TODD

- **Take mental mini-breaks throughout the day.** Before entering a meeting or making an important phone call, I try to remind myself to take a few deep breaths to sharpen my focus. Science backs me up: I'm getting more oxygen to my brain, and thus will have an easier time focusing. Many of us unconsciously hold our breath or breathe more shallowly during stress, and the more cognizant you are of that, the more oxygenated your brain and body will be— thus helping to sustain your energy.

- **Be proactive about scheduling a longer mental break.** I regularly plan what I call an "ego day," which means going to a different setting to think and reflect. (Todd calls it a "me day"; Scott calls it a "corporate retreat for one.") It doesn't have to be at a luxury spa; my parents' empty kitchen was once the site of a brilliant ego day. Check in with yourself: Are you on track with the goals and targets you've set? Are you headed in the right direction? If you're heading into an extremely hectic period, try to proactively schedule an ego day afterward. That's the key: if you don't plan them, they won't happen.

- **Learn new things.** Investing in yourself is not just about how you recover, but how you grow. Certain types of learning can be both relaxing and rewarding. Pursue a new interest or skill that might take some time to develop. This stretches your mental capability, making you more multidimensional in the process. Try learning the basics of a new language, writing a book, or taking a class. Scott once told me about a friend who attended a professional conference—only to realize that she'd gone to the wrong room and was accidentally attending a presentation on high-performance boat engines. She enjoyed this unexpected detour so much that she made it an annual tradition to attend a workshop on a new topic. What a fun idea—I've registered Scott for an anime conference in Moscow next winter.

- **Your own best advice to yourself:**

Connect

- **Volunteer.** Consider giving back to your community and those in need.

- **Invest in your social network.** Your social relationships help you grow and develop. Surround yourself with people who give you energy rather than drain it. Reflect on your "friend list"—maybe it's time to declutter it.

- **Create special moments.** When someone in our family has a birthday, we always have birthday events rather than giving gifts. We've done a pottery class, horseback riding—anything we haven't tried before. It becomes an opportunity to explore and see new things together. Could you do something similar with your family and friends—or even your team?

- **Reach out to someone in need.** When I'm stressed out or feeling down, I like to reach out to someone who might be in a more challenging situation than me, and ask how I can help. It puts my own challenges into perspective; but most important, it makes them feel better, and it might be a chance to rejuvenate a neglected relationship.

- **Your own best advice to yourself:**

_____

_____

Move

- **Treat exercise as a luxury.** It's easy to think of exercise as a must. And you do have to do it, because your life depends on how much you move. But instead of thinking of it as a chore, I look at it in a different way: I _get_ to do this luxurious, one-hour yoga session, or whatever it is. I changed my paradigm from "exercise is drudgery" to "exercise is my special time." It's a way to treat myself.

- **Think outside the gym.** Exercise doesn't need to just happen in the gym. Research shows that it's not how much time you spend there that counts, but how much movement you incorporate into your everyday life. So get up and move from your desk. During my client work sessions, I ask my participants to stand up in the middle of class to do ten squats. That is a true energy boost!

- **Use technology.** You can use some brilliant apps for a quick workout. All it takes is twenty minutes to feed your brain with focus, energy, and happy thoughts.

- **Get your heart pumping.** When it comes to mental and overall health, working out creates stamina and better results. Pick any activity you enjoy that increases your pulse.

- **Find your people.** Having a training partner increases the likelihood that you'll actually work out. Combine exercise with your role as a friend, partner, or parent. I do yoga and badminton with my daughters, run with my friend (time that also doubles as peer coaching), and have been part of online communities when my training needed a little motivational push.

- **Your own best advice to yourself:**

_____

_____

Eat

- **Remember the main purpose of eating is to fuel yourself with energy.** We eat to boost brainpower, not just to satisfy hunger. The next time you're choosing what to eat, ask, "Which of these choices will give me more energy?" For example, whole foods will sustain you longer than processed foods, fruits and nuts will keep you better focused than quick-hit carbohydrates, etc.

- **Inventory your food choices last week.** Generally, how much of your diet consisted of energy-sustaining foods vs. energy-depleting foods? If you're not where you want to be, try one of the great tools and apps that track your nutrition.

- **Make your own "fast food."** Store healthy snacks in your desk, locker, or bag. If you go to the trouble of bringing it and have it right in front of you, you're less likely to sneak a bite of the leftover birthday cake in the break room.

- **Hold healthy lunch meetings.** If your Tuesday lunch is catching up with a peer over a hearty salad, you're scoring a win–win of social connection and energy-boosting eating—much better than eating cold pizza alone at your desk.

- **Prepare for the postwork hunger.** You'll likely be most tired and vulnerable to bad choices after work. At home, have healthy snacks ready so when you walk in the door, you don't end up at the bottom of a potato-chip bag.

- **Your own best advice to yourself:**

  _____

  _____

Would you add another energy driver to your list? When you're under stress, which energy driver do you crave the most? Which one is your go-to driver? Which one do you avoid?

Take a long-term approach to managing your energy. You'll most likely have times at work and home that will be more hectic than others. Our colleague Roger Merrill, coauthor of the time-management book *First Things First,* calls these moments "seasons of imbalance." You can probably think of a few: tax season for accountants, welcoming a new child for parents, back to school for educators. These can be some of the most exciting times in life—and they're also exhausting. During those times, we cut out certain priorities and goals to survive (and gym time is usually the first to go).

After everything calms down, we often forget to *bring back* those other priorities. Before you know it, imbalance becomes your new normal, even though it might not be necessary or sustainable. Catching yourself as you transition out of a busy period is difficult but extremely important to reinstate your healthy habits. Go back to the gym, spend time coaching a certain team member, or eat a proper lunch away from your desk.

Remember my example earlier in this chapter of starting a new job and finding myself at the office too early? I did work intensively, even after the six-month mark, and cut out several tasks in my life to focus on the most important ones. But that didn't mean I never went back to the gym. While it didn't fit into my life during that period, I have since had much more time to invest in myself. My daughters are now teenagers, and I've been able to run half marathons and become a yoga instructor. Recently Scott interviewed famed fitness and goal-achievement expert Jillian Michaels, who reinforced the idea that people *can* have it all, just not at the same time.

Seasons of imbalance are okay as long as they stay seasons. The problem is when the season turns into a *lifestyle*. Keep an eye out for temporary periods of stress that have no end point.

TRY IT OUT ⟳

Stop/Start/Continue

Did you disagree with anything you read in this section? Do you feel like you are too busy to take time for yourself?

Look through your energy audit and the tips we shared. Think about what gives you energy and what drains it. What is one thing that, starting today, you can stop, start, and continue to keep up your energy?

As a leader, it starts with you. If you want your brain to use its full potential, you need to fuel it with energy. And just as you want to honor commitments to other people, you want to honor your commitments to yourself.

—TODD

SKILL 2: MANAGE YOUR TIME

We've noticed a huge shift in time management in the past decade. We used to teach people how to distinguish between high and low priorities and help them identify and cut deadweight out of their schedules. But now people are deciding between competing priorities, all of which are important. We at FranklinCovey have termed this new leadership competency "decision management." Unfortunately, there aren't many time-wasters to eliminate; rather, it's about somehow choosing between landing an important project, coaching a distraught team member, and making it home for family dinner—all vitally important.

Many of us spend our time and energy reacting to whatever stress, demands, or urgencies come our way—whether or not they help us achieve our highest priorities. Todd calls this defeating tendency "the pinball syndrome" in his book *Get Better*. Managing time in this environment is as much about choosing what *not to do* as choosing what *to do*. You'll need to discern what is important, then have the courage to say "no" or "not now" to what isn't—which is uncomfortable and at times even risky.

Define the leader you want to be. To know what to say no to, you must first define your big *yes*—what's most important to you. Years from now, what do you wish your team would say about you? What are your leadership values and priorities?

Choose your priorities—and share them. You're probably not going to have a problem coming up with important ways to fill your days. Just reading this book has hopefully given you lots of ideas; but that may feel overwhelming if you don't have a way to fit them into your jam-packed calendar.

Carefully pick your priorities and, equally important, decide what *not* to do. Once you choose your priorities, do your very best to stick to them. When you are in the midst of the whirlwind of day-to-day urgencies, you have to keep to your plan in order to achieve your goals. One of the downsides of being an effective leader is that your colleagues, boss, and team will come to you asking for input, support, and new projects. The only person protecting your own time is most likely going to be you.

I find that the easiest way for me to say no to things is if I'm 100 percent clear on what I'm spending my time on instead, and *why*. Being able to articulate that "why" to others will help you maintain healthy relationships.

Sharing your priorities and goals is a great thing to do, not only when being asked for help, but in general. Once said out loud, they become more real, to yourself and others. As we discussed in earlier practices, you don't want your priorities to be a secret from your team. Many of your priorities should be aligned with their priorities in one way or another.

Stay flexible when urgencies arise. Even if you've carefully structured your time, the day will not go as planned and urgencies will arise—more or less depending on the nature of your work. So leave some space in your schedule for unexpected emergencies. The percentage will vary by your industry, role, and manager. But if you have taken the time to plan, you have a center line to return to after the fire is out.

Avoid the two ends of the spectrum: being so rigid that you can't cope with a change in plans, or being addicted to urgencies—even creating them. Remind yourself to have nimbleness and fluidity so if your boss texts, you're not so inflexible that it craters your day. On the other hand, don't be too attracted to those urgencies; for example, treating *any* email with a red exclamation point as urgent when it might not actually be. We want to be malleable but not invite urgencies in. When a curve ball is thrown our way, we should consider our priorities and make a choice to respond either in the affirmative, or with a respectful "I can do that at a later time, but not right now."

Make time for your priorities through weekly planning. It sounds counterintuitive to spend more time on planning if you're already so busy you can't even get your most important work done. But if you don't plan your week, you're at the mercy of the winds of change, reacting to what comes your way instead of deciding what's important and what you want to accomplish.

We like the "big rocks" and "gravel" metaphor originally popularized in *The 7 Habits of Highly Effective People*. Many of you may have seen the viral video of Dr. Stephen R. Covey challenging an audience participant to fit all of their priorities (symbolized as rocks) into a jar of gravel. The larger rocks in the jar represent the most important actions you commit to weekly to achieve your key priorities. The gravel is everything else. At the beginning of each week, put the "Big Rocks" (your personal and professional priorities based on your values) in your schedule first and let the gravel (smaller tasks and minutiae) fill in the schedule around them. Otherwise, if you put the small tasks in first, they will fill up the schedule, leaving no room for the Big Rocks.

TRY IT OUT ✪

Schedule Your Priorities

Think about your priorities and goals. What specific actions can you do this week to help you achieve them? Put those "Big Rocks" in your calendar.

Review the previous practices. What skills and practices could be most helpful in reaching your goals? Put them in your calendar as your leadership "Big Rocks."

—TODD

Having coached many leaders on how to make the best use of their time, I find that many don't use the full potential of their planning system. Many leaders just use it for their meetings. An example of a typical manager's weekly calendar could look like this:

Weekly Schedule Example: Traditional View

	MONDAY	TUESDAY	WEDNESDAY	THURSDAY	FRIDAY
6–8 a.m.					
8–10 a.m.			1-on-1		
10 a.m.– 12 p.m.	Team meeting		Client meeting	Management meeting	
12–2 p.m.		Lunch with client			
2–4 p.m.	Meet with IT		1-on-1		
4–6 p.m.	Meet with my manager				
6–8 p.m.					
8–10 p.m.					

What is the main problem with this calendar view? To me, it *appears* that you have quite a lot of free time and are available for urgencies (and more meetings!). But that's probably not the case. I bet your week is pretty full, despite your calendar not reflecting it.

So, what should be on your calendar besides meetings? Your Big Rocks for the week, to start; then other important (but maybe not urgent) priorities like strategic thinking or industry research. Then you should add things that you know from experience will take time. For example, travel time for your client meetings, documenting your notes after you meet with your manager, and preparing for your 1-on-1s. Make sure you master the art of prepopulating your calendar with your commitments and priorities.

Think about when your best energy flow is, and proactively try to build that into your way of working. When would be the best time for meetings? When would be the best time for focused or introverted work?

A more effective leader's schedule could look like this:

Weekly Schedule Example: Effective View

	MONDAY	TUESDAY	WEDNESDAY	THURSDAY	FRIDAY
6–8 a.m.		Morning run		Morning run	Morning yoga
8–10 a.m.	Prepare and research for this week's client meetings	Morning at home	1-on-1s	Focused work on important project	
10 a.m.–12 p.m.	Team accountability meeting	Focused work on important project	Travel to client meeting/Client meeting	Management meeting	Team coaching on new process
12–2 p.m.	Travel to lunch (call Mom!)/Lunch with client	Doctor's appointment	Walk-and-talk meeting	Lunch with peer to get feedback	Friday team lunch
2–4 p.m.	Meet with IT manager to learn about new process	Follow up from lunch client meeting	1-on-1s	Prepare team coaching session	Prepare team meetings and 1-on-1s for next week
4–6 p.m.	Meet with my manager			Weekly planning for next week	
6–8 p.m.	Family time/activities	Work late night	Family time/activities	Work late night	Date night
8–10 p.m.			Evening yoga		

This second view gives a more accurate picture of how much time you have available for last-minute urgencies. And remember, putting renewing activities such as exercise into your calendar increases the likelihood of it happening.

You might be in an environment where you never need to work late: congratulations! But if you are, be proactive and schedule those evenings in advance. My mother gave me this advice early in my career: plan for a late night at the office once a week to finish off important tasks. If you don't have to worry about leaving the office by a certain time, you can feel more in control. You can then choose to leave early another day when you are more needed at home or want to invest time for yourself.

Decide what you can say no to. Once you have this more realistic view of your week, it will be a little easier to say no. You won't get ahead by addressing the gravel first and hoping you'll get to the Big Rocks later. Instead, you must decide what is most important and plan your time around those activities. You have to say no to some of the gravel—and you might even have to choose between some of your Big Rocks.

As you go through the week, ask yourself these questions when deciding what to spend time on:

- *What's the potential payoff?* If a task has significant long-term impact, address it now, even if it doesn't seem urgent in the moment.

- *Will this task help my team, company, or me meet an important goal?* If helping a direct report speeds up progress on a strategic project, it's probably worth dropping everything to do it.

- *Can it wait?* If it can, perhaps let it. But determine how long it can wait before it becomes a crisis. Address it before this point.

- *Should I be the one to do this?* If there's someone with more experience or who could use the chance to learn, maybe it's time to delegate. See Practice 3: Set Up Your Team to Get Results for more information.

- *Is this on my schedule because it's comfortable or easy?* If you're filling your week with quick-win tasks that make you feel like you're accomplishing things, you might just be running in place.

- *Is this my priority—or someone else's?* As with all innovation, there are upsides and downsides to our digital calendars. Allowing colleagues to view our calendars has created enormous efficiency in scheduling meetings for busy people. The downside is that many people can view your availability and send you appointments, making you feel compelled or culturally obliged to accept them. You may want to block out segments of time with titles that won't be challenged by a colleague sending an invite.

Plan daily. In addition to thirty minutes of weekly planning, effective leaders invest at least some time each day to thoughtful planning. Take ten minutes to modify your plan based on current conditions. How are you feeling that day? What did you accomplish earlier in the week? Have your "Big Rock" priorities changed? Look at your goals for the week: What activities can you undertake that will change those from goals to accomplishments by the end of your workweek?

Daily planning protects those priorities you identified at the start of the week from productivity-killing minutiae. But even with the best intentions, you might get pulled away for an emergency or an important task that takes longer than anticipated. That's why it's important to revisit your priorities each day and adapt as needed.

Once you block out time for important tasks, fill in the rest of your calendar with the gravel, like updating meetings and answering email. Remember your energy and focus needs, and proactively schedule some breaks or time to chat with a colleague—that allows you to mentally refresh, while preventing your break from turning into a forty-five-minute speaking tour with the whole office.

Once you finish your daily planning, dive into your highest-priority tasks. Do it before distractions and urgencies fragment your attention.

SKILL 3: COACH YOUR TEAM TO MANAGE THEIR TIME AND ENERGY

Beyond your own quest for balance, you need to coach your team to create it for themselves too. Just as you are responsible for the results of your team, you are also in some ways responsible for the energy of the team. Leaders need to be mindful of when creativity has lapsed or when people simply need a break to recharge. Many leaders underestimate their impact on the team's energy levels.

Perhaps you feel skeptical about your role in managing your team members' energy. Isn't it their responsibility to take care of their health and energy levels? Does the energy of your team *really* matter? Absolutely. You can't force-feed your team vitamins, put them on a treadmill, or balance their lives. But you can model a healthy lifestyle and be mindful of when you're depleting their energy levels with relentless demands for overtime, unrealistic deadlines, and saying yes to too many projects. You'll have a greater influence on their energy by what you model and how well you live the skills in this section.

Here are our best practices for managing the energy of your team.

BE A ROLE MODEL

As a leader, your behavior by default becomes the standard for everyone else. If you come in early, your team is going to feel they need to beat you there. If you stay until 8 p.m., few people will dare to tiptoe past your office at 5 p.m.

Unless you deliberately, clearly, and repeatedly set expectations, your team will interpret how *you* work as how *they* should work. The problem is your habits might actually reduce their effectiveness. Your night owls (about 20 percent of the population, according to Daniel Pink, so possibly 20 percent of your team as well)* will be yawning over their laptops at 7 a.m. Employees in a different time zone might be sacrificing personal time for meetings during your peak.

Last year I was delivering a keynote address to over a thousand people at a large, publicly held women's clothing company. I'd talked with the CEO and her executive team weeks earlier to ensure the message I was delivering was what they needed. The CEO was clear that I had an hour and fifteen minutes, so I had organized my keynote around that time frame.

The presentation went well, and the audience was engaged. They were so engaged that some of their responses throughout the keynote ended up cutting into some of the time I'd allowed. With about three minutes to go, I said, "I have one final concept that will take about five minutes, so we will be about two minutes over. Is that okay with everyone?" I was confident that I would get a resounding yes. Well, whether they said yes or not, I don't remember, because as I glanced at the CEO in the front row, she was subtly waving her finger and mouthing the word "no."

I quickly made a joke and said, "On second thought, we are going to end right on time," and everyone laughed while I finished the keynote.

---

* Mejia, Z. (2018, April 30). How to Time Your Day for Peak Performance, Based on Your Chronotype. Retrieved from https://www.cnbc.com/2018/04/30/daniel-pink -how-to-time-your-day-for-peak-performance.html.

Afterward the CEO came up to me and said how pleased she was with the presentation. Then the CEO demonstrated why she is such an extraordinary leader and responsible for such a successful organization. She said, "I'm sorry you weren't able to go over the time allowed, but one of our core values is respect for our employees' time. And one of the ways we model that is my commitment that all meetings will start and end on time, no exceptions."

Wow, I was so impressed. I thanked her for the opportunity and how she truly led by example. No wonder everyone I spoke with at this organization commented on her extraordinary leadership. Managing your time really matters and makes a difference in your results. So does walking your talk!

—TODD

CREATE MORE ENERGY

Have you ever entered a meeting and noticed that everyone on your team seems drained? One person is recovering from the flu, another had a bad incident at home, and a third is struggling with a stretch assignment. And here you are, trying to kick off an important project. And on top of it, you didn't sleep that well last night . . .

This is the moment you need to remind yourself that you are the leader. Do you want your team to walk out of this meeting the way they entered (or, horrid thought, even more drained)? Or can you use this as an opportunity to infuse some positive energy so that your team can go out into the world with renewed enthusiasm?

I try to see it as a positive challenge whenever I find myself in those situations. I might start with a quick celebration of how we're making a difference, or some other good news. I also talk openly with the team about what kind of meeting we want to have, how our time together could build or drain our energy, and everyone's role in creating that.

In your meetings, pay attention to the task at hand and your team's energy level. If you sense a gap, set the tone, pace, and engagement level. Don't think you need to be the cheerleader and muster up the energy for everyone. Instead, simple activities can boost energy, like beginning the meeting with quick life updates from volunteers, asking everyone to stand up, or getting into pairs to brainstorm about a solution to a key project.

CREATE A CHANCE TO CONNECT

In our discussion on the 5 Energy Drivers, we talked about how important it is to connect with others. As a leader, you can facilitate that connection—and that doesn't necessarily require off-site retreats or elaborate team-building activities.

In many organizations, sharing anything personal with your team used to be frowned upon, but this is changing radically. Today's workforce is much more integrated in terms of personal and professional lives. And in many cases, we spend as much time (or more) with our colleagues as with our family and friends.

So it's increasingly beneficial to team culture and productivity to foster a deeper sense of connection between you and your team. Simple tricks at your office can make all the difference. Consider creating team breakfasts or taking turns letting everyone share a special interest each week.

CHALLENGE YOUR PARADIGM

When I was managing a large department, a talented new graduate joined my team. At our introduction meeting, she said, "Just to let you know, I'm not really a morning person, so it's better if I come in after ten." I was like, "Um . . . no!" I'm an early bird. I like being in the office at seven, so even though I never said it out loud, I used to believe that slackers came in at nine. I wish I could say that I was open to change, but I was completely inflexible with this new hire.

And now I ask myself why. She didn't want to work less; she just wanted to work differently. She was probably brilliant in the evening. Of course there would be days when she was required to be there by nine, but other days, why not? Why was I so inflexible? Just because her style wasn't mine didn't mean I couldn't accommodate it.

With a significant shift in the workforce, established organizations will be challenged to take into consideration the flow and best energies of their employees, probably to everyone's advantage. So I would encourage you to challenge your mindset in how you and your team work to achieve highest results. Of course there are certain roles, like customer-facing ones, where you have to be at a certain place at a certain time. But customers change their preferences too. Could a new way of work even enhance your offering?

Leaders choose how they want to live their lives—and for some, work is their top priority. That's fine, but they also expect that of their team, whether or not their employees have the same priorities.

You can say over and over, "You don't have to stay late just because I do." But your people will feel like they're letting you down if they're not doing what you're modeling.

Have a frank discussion with your team about the importance of balance. While leaders should have expectations around results, your team achieves results in different ways. Some of us accomplish things sporadically throughout the day, and others get things done in a concentrated period of time. One of my employees, for example, attends his daughter's soccer practice every Tuesday afternoon—no problem, because he always has his reports in by the end of the day. Stay focused on results, not necessarily the methods.

—TODD

FINAL THOUGHT: YOU DON'T BURN OUT WITHOUT FIRST BEING ON FIRE

We often expect disengaged team members to burn out, but more often it's the opposite. It's the engaged ones who are most at risk—people who feel so passionate about what they do that they can't stop themselves from taking on too much. They start to lose track of what's really a high priority, or their leaders haven't given them direction about what to say no to.

I had an overachiever on my team who would excitedly share what she was doing during our 1-on-1s, and I felt that there wasn't much I needed to do. But she suddenly went from super engaged to saying, "I'm not sure I can do this any longer."

I realized she needed my support and coaching to identify her most important Big Rocks. We spent her 1-on-1s the following months reviewing her weekly planning and prioritizing. I've been lucky to have these brilliant, ambitious, hardworking people on my team, and it's tempting to delegate to them because they gladly take everything on. But if you want to help them channel their passion and use it on the right things, help them prioritize: How are you going to use your limited time next week? Of all these great things you could do, which are most important? Which are your Big Rocks and what do you need to cut out—at least for now? That will prevent them from hitting the proverbial wall.

Take a moment to review this practice, and note the insights that most resonated with you.

_____

_____

_____

_____

_____

_____

_____

_____

Jot down two to three action items you want to commit to.

_____

_____

_____

_____

_____

_____

_____

_____

CONCLUSION

As Todd so insightfully asked in the introduction, do you want to be a great leader, or do you want your team to be led by a great leader? Similarly, researcher and leadership expert Liz Wiseman asks, "Are you the genius in the room or the genius *maker*?" To me, this is one of the most insightful questions in leadership. You can't be both at the same time—you have to choose.

Leaders with enduring careers are genius makers, we'd argue. You have to figure out what kind of leader your people need, which could be different from the leader you might have been trying to be.

Do you know what your team needs? Do you care? Are you asking? Are you attuned to it? This comes with flexibility, empathy, and listening. The future leader is nimble, not with their values and ethics, but in their style and skills. They identify the leadership competencies their people need, then grow their skills and maturity to match that.

One of my first-level leaders had an incalculable impact on my career. I was a newly hired recruiter, and it was my thirty-fifth day on the job. She walked me up to one of the senior leaders and said, "I want to introduce you to Todd Davis. Let me tell you what he's accomplished in his first month of employment." I panicked. What was she going to say? Was she going to ask me to say something, because I couldn't think of one single thing I'd accomplished yet!

She went on to list the sales positions I'd filled, the relocation policy I'd written, and the recruitment strategy I'd drafted. I couldn't believe she'd taken such an interest in my work.

I don't share that experience because I think I'm so wonderful; I share it because my manager noticed. She believed in me way more than I believed in myself. That moment shaped my career and confidence for the next several years.

The power of someone sincerely believing in you can change the course of your career.

Yes, leadership is daunting. But you can make a real difference not only in people's careers, but in their lives.

—TODD

Recently I ran into a former employee whom I'd worked with a decade prior. She said, "Victoria, there's something I always remember about you. When I was fairly new to your team, we were discussing some issue, and you said, 'This will be important when you become the director of learning and development.' I had never thought of myself as a future director, and you said it like it was the most natural thing in the world. It changed my paradigm that, yes, I can become a director one day." She teared up and said, "Now here I am, the director of learning and development for this large organization. And you saw that."

It was quite an emotional moment for her, but even more for me. I truly believe that everyone deserves a great manager. If we choose to be a leader, we should do our utmost to be a great one, because we can make a difference in people's lives.

At the same time, that doesn't mean everyone on your team will always love you. There will be tough moments, and your particular style and personality might not be everyone's perfect fit. Don't beat yourself up too much about that.

Use the practices, insights, and ideas you get from reading this book, then go out and top it off with your own unique style. Your people will find you. You will make a difference.

—VICTORIA

This is not something you're going to achieve by tomorrow. Release yourself from the anxiety that by next Friday you're going to master all 6 Practices. Todd, Victoria, and I took decades to truly implement them, and even now we help course-correct each other.

Becoming a great leader takes time, repetition, successes, and failures—they're all equal parts of the formula. So relax, and give yourself some space. It's a journey, and we can tell you: it's worth it.

IT'S TIME TO STOP READING
AND START DOING

We're thrilled that you've joined us for this journey. We feel passionate about helping first-level leaders (and for that matter, leaders at every level) not only learn these practices, but also bring them to life. As we reach the final pages of this book, let's talk about how you can take your insights and make real, sustainable improvements to your leadership, starting today.

The exercises on the following pages show you how to put the 6 Practices together, one step at a time. We ask you to revisit the insights and action items you noted at the end of each chapter and create an action plan customized for you. Then you'll bring it all together in the next section, "My Plan for Becoming the Great Manager My Team Deserves."

PRACTICE 1: DEVELOP A LEADER'S MINDSET

Sum up your key insights from this practice:

_____

_____

_____

Identify how you could change your mindset around this practice:

_____

_____

_____

Check which actions you want to take, then schedule them.

☐ Review your mindsets using the exercises on page 12.

☐ Use the "Getting to Know Your Team" tool on page 22.

Your ideas for additional actions:

☐ _____

☐ _____

☐ _____

PRACTICE 2: HOLD REGULAR 1-ON-1S

Sum up your key insights from this practice:

_____

_____

_____

Identify how you could change your mindset around this practice:

_____

_____

_____

Check which actions you want to take, then schedule them.

- ❏ Analyze the levels of engagement on your team using the six-level framework on page 27.
- ❏ Create the 1-on-1 structure that works best for your team.
- ❏ Share your intentions and the theory behind 1-on-1s with your team.
- ❏ Book recurring calendar appointments for your 1-on-1s.
- ❏ Prepare for your first meeting using the planner on page 46 and the coaching questions on page 49.
- ❏ After a few 1-on-1s, ask your team members for feedback on the value of the meetings and how well you're listening and coaching.

Your ideas for additional actions:

- ❏ _____
- ❏ _____
- ❏ _____

PRACTICE 3: SET UP YOUR TEAM TO GET RESULTS

Sum up your key insights from this practice:

_____

_____

_____

Identify how you could change your mindset around this practice:

_____

_____

_____

Check which actions you want to take, then schedule them.

- ❏ Meet with your manager to understand their goals and the goals they want your team to accomplish. Learn how those align with the organization's priorities.

- ❏ Call a team meeting to clarify your goals. Announce the purpose and structure of your weekly team-accountability meetings.

- ❏ Create a scoreboard to track progress toward your goals. Assign someone to update it weekly.

- ❏ Consider what tasks could be delegated to other team members. Pay particular attention to tasks that can stretch and grow your team members' capacity. Delegate the work to them using the framework on page 66, and follow up in your 1-on-1s.

- ❏ Schedule and hold a weekly fifteen- to twenty-minute team-accountability meeting to review progress on the scoreboard.

- ❏ When you achieve the goal, celebrate—and go as big as you can.

Your ideas for additional actions:

- ❏ _____
- ❏ _____
- ❏ _____

PRACTICE 4: CREATE A CULTURE OF FEEDBACK

Sum up your key insights from this practice:

_____

_____

_____

Identify how you could change your mindset around this practice:

_____

_____

_____

Check which actions you want to take, then schedule them.

- ❏ Reflect on whether you have a tendency toward high courage or high consideration. Are there any situations, people, or contexts where you need to rebalance?

- ❏ Call your team together and announce your intentions to increase the amount of feedback you give and seek.

- ❏ Use the Feedback Planner tool on page 105 to deliver feedback as the need arises. Role-play any particularly difficult conversations in advance.

- ❏ Seek feedback from at least one person over the next month. Use the six steps on page 102.

Your ideas for additional actions:

- ❏ _____
- ❏ _____
- ❏ _____

PRACTICE 5: LEAD THROUGH CHANGE

Sum up your key insights from this practice:

_____

_____

_____

Identify how you could change your mindset around this practice:

_____

_____

_____

Check which actions you want to take, then schedule them.

Before your next change initiative:

❏ Reflect on your tolerance for change using the questions on page 116.

During your next change initiative:

❏ If you're not fully on board with the change, meet with your manager to gain better context.

❏ Announce the change using the planner on page 138 and the best practices in Skill 1.

❏ Check in with your team members during their 1-on-1s.

❏ Create new goals and scoreboards, if necessary.

❏ Celebrate early wins.

After your next change initiative:

❏ Seek feedback on how to better lead change during your 1-on-1s. Use the questions on page 134.

Your ideas for additional actions:

❏ _____

❏ _____

❏ _____

PRACTICE 6: MANAGE YOUR TIME AND ENERGY

Sum up your key insights from this practice:

_____

_____

_____

Identify how you could change your mindset around this practice:

_____

_____

_____

Check which actions you want to take, then schedule them.

- ❏ Assess your energy needs using the questions on page 147. Adjust your schedule to align with those needs, if possible.

- ❏ Do a personal energy audit on page 149. Identify which driver to work on and one thing you can stop, start, and continue doing to improve that driver.

- ❏ Book a recurring thirty-minute appointment to plan your week.

- ❏ Get into the habit of spending five to fifteen minutes on daily planning.

- ❏ Try increasing the energy of an upcoming meeting using the suggestions on page 166.

Your ideas for additional actions:

- ❏ _____
- ❏ _____
- ❏ _____

MY PLAN FOR BECOMING THE
GREAT MANAGER MY TEAM DESERVES

Date: _____

What kind of manager does my team need right now? What kind
of manager does my organization need me to be?

_____

_____

_____

What would I have to change to become the manager they deserve?

_____

_____

_____

Fast-forward ten years and look back to this moment. What do I
want my team to say about this time in their lives? What results do
I want to have delivered? How do I want my team to describe my
leadership?

_____

_____

_____

What do I need to do in the coming months to make that vision
happen?

_____

_____

_____

What obstacles might get in the way of building my leadership reputation, and how will I overcome them?

_____

_____

_____

How will I hold myself accountable to this vision?

_____

_____

_____

When will I assess my progress and determine adjustments in the coming weeks and months?

_____

_____

_____

INDEX

Page numbers in *italics* refer to illustrations.

About FranklinCovey

FranklinCovey is a global, public company specializing in organizational-performance improvement. We help organizations and individuals achieve results that require a change in human behavior. Our expertise is in seven areas: leadership, execution, productivity, trust, sales performance, customer loyalty, and education. FranklinCovey clients have included 90 percent of the *Fortune*® 100, more than 75 percent of the *Fortune*® 500, thousands of small and mid-size businesses, as well as numerous government entities and educational institutions. FranklinCovey has more than 100 direct and partner offices providing professional services in more than 160 countries and territories.

ABOUT THE AUTHORS

Scott Miller serves as FranklinCovey's executive vice president of thought leadership. He is the host of *On Leadership with Scott Miller*, a weekly leadership webcast, podcast, and newsletter that features interviews with renowned business titans, authors, and experts. Scott also writes a weekly leadership column for Inc.com and is a regular contributor to Arianna Huffington's Thrive Global and the *American City Business Journal*. He is the author of FranklinCovey's *Management Mess to Leadership Success: 30 Challenges to Become the Leader You Would Follow*.

In his previous roles as executive vice president of business development and chief marketing officer, Scott led the global transformation of FranklinCovey's brand. Prior to that, he served as general manager of client facilitation services and general manager of FranklinCovey's central region. Scott joined the Covey Leadership Center in 1996 as a client partner with the Education division.

Scott began his professional career in 1992 with the Disney Development Company as a founding member of the development team that designed the town of Celebration, Florida. Scott now lives in Salt Lake City, Utah, with his wife and three young sons.

Todd Davis is FranklinCovey's chief people officer and the bestselling author of *Get Better: 15 Proven Practices to Build Effective Relationships at Work*.

Todd has more than 30 years of experience in human resources, talent development, executive recruiting, sales, and marketing. He has been with FranklinCovey for more than two decades, and is currently responsible for global talent development of employees in more than 40 offices reaching 160 countries.

Todd led the development of many of FranklinCovey's core offerings and world-renowned content. He has delivered keynote addresses at leading conferences such as the World Business Forum, the Chief

Learning Officer Symposium, the Association for Talent Development, and HR.com.

As a respected global thought leader, Todd has been featured in *Inc.*, *Fast Company*, *Harvard Business Review*, and Thrive Global.

Todd has served on HR.com's Advisory Board for the Institute of Human Resources, and is a member of the Association for Talent Development and the Society for Human Resource Management. Todd and his family reside in Holladay, Utah.

Victoria Roos Olsson is a senior leadership consultant at FranklinCovey. She is an expert in leadership development and has trained, developed, and coached managers around the world for the past twenty years. She has also led learning and development divisions for large corporations in Europe and the Middle East, including Jumeirah and Hilton.

Victoria is an experienced keynote speaker who engages her audience, whether twenty or two thousand people are in the room. She is an expert facilitator of several FranklinCovey offerings, and served on the developing team for *The 7 Habits of Highly Effective People* and *The 4 Essential Roles of Leadership* programs. She effortlessly combines enthusiasm with focus and drive, helping leadership teams achieve their desired results.

Victoria is a native Swede and has a bachelor's degree in economics and hotel management from the renowned Hotelschool The Hague in the Netherlands.

Victoria is passionate about holistic leadership and draws on her expertise as a certified yoga instructor and running coach. An additional passion project is the podcast *Roos&Shine* that she hosts with her sister, with listeners in more than seventy countries. Victoria leads an international life with her husband and two daughters.

THE CHALLENGE FOR FIRST-LEVEL LEADERS

PARTICIPATE IN *THE 6 CRITICAL PRACTICES FOR LEADING A TEAM*™ WORK SESSION

The role of the first-level leader has always been tough and today's realities make the role even tougher. People skills typically account for 80 percent of success in this role.

Yet many people are promoted because of their technical capabilities. Both new and experienced first-level leaders can struggle when it comes to excelling at leading teams in today's workplace.

This work session helps first-level leaders:

- Fast-track their development as emerging leaders.
- Learn the basic skills and tools every manager needs, but few receive.

For more information, visit
FRANKLINCOVEY.COM/SOLUTIONS/ 6-CRITICAL-PRACTICES.HTML

THE ULTIMATE COMPETITIVE ADVANTAGE

FranklinCovey
ALL ACCESS PASS

The FranklinCovey All Access Pass provides unlimited access to our best-in-class content and solutions, allowing you to expand your reach, achieve your business objectives, and sustainably impact performance across your organization.

AS A PASSHOLDER, YOU CAN:

- Access FranklinCovey's world-class content, whenever and wherever you need it, including *The 7 Habits of Highly Effective People®: Signature Edition 4.0*, Leading at the *Speed of Trust®*, and *The 5 Choices to Extraordinary Productivity®*.

- Certify your internal facilitators to teach our content, deploy FranklinCovey consultants, or use digital content to reach your learners with the behavior-changing content you require.

- Have access to a certified implementation specialist who will help design impact journeys for behavior change.

- Organize FranklinCovey content around your specific business-related needs.

- Build a common learning experience throughout your entire global organization with our core-content areas, localized into 16 languages.

Join thousands of organizations using the All Access Pass to implement strategy, close operational gaps, increase sales, drive customer loyalty, and improve employee engagement.

To learn more, visit
FRANKLINCOVEY.COM

FranklinCovey
THE ULTIMATE COMPETITIVE ADVANTAGE

FRANKLINCOVEY
ONLEADERSHIP
WITH
SCOTT MILLER

Join FranklinCovey's executive vice president Scott Miller for weekly interviews with thought leaders, bestselling authors, and world-renowned experts in the areas of organizational culture, leadership development, execution, and personal productivity. Delivered to your inbox via email newsletter or on the go as a podcast.

SUBSCRIBE TO THE *ON LEADERSHIP* NEWSLETTER, AND ACCESS INTERVIEWS WITH:

STEPHEN M. R. COVEY
AUTHOR, *THE SPEED OF TRUST*

STEPHANIE McMAHON
CHIEF BRAND OFFICER, WWE

GRETCHEN RUBIN
AUTHOR, *THE HAPPINESS PROJECT*

TODD DAVIS
AUTHOR, *GET BETTER*

DORIS KEARNS GOODWIN
PULITZER PRIZE-WINNING HISTORIAN

GENERAL STANLEY McCHRYSTAL
RETIRED FOUR-STAR GENERAL

CHRIS McCHESNEY
EXPERT, STRATEGY EXECUTION

SUSAN CAIN
AUTHOR, *QUIET*

LIZ WISEMAN
AUTHOR, *MULTIPLIERS*

GUY KAWASAKI
AUTHOR, *WISE GUY*

Subscribe to the email newsletter and podcast at
FRANKLINCOVEY.COM/ONLEADERSHIP

SCHEDULE AN AUTHOR
TO SPEAK AT YOUR EVENT

SCOTT MILLER   TODD DAVIS   VICTORIA ROOS OLSSON

Are you planning an event for your organization? Schedule an author to deliver an engaging keynote speech tailor-made for today's leaders at events including:

- Association and Industry Conferences
- Sales Conferences
- Executive and Board Retreats

- Annual Meetings
- Company Functions
- Onsite Consulting
- Client Engagements

These authors have spoken at hundreds of conferences and client events worldwide.

To schedule a bestselling author today
visit **franklincovey.com**

THE ULTIMATE COMPETITIVE ADVANTAGE

READ MORE
FROM THE LEADERSHIP EXPERTS AT FRANKLINCOVEY

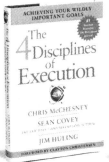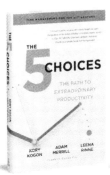

MORE THAN 40 MILLION COPIES SOLD

Learn more about how to develop yourself personally, lead your team, or transform your organization with these bestselling books, by visiting **franklincovey.com/books.html**

THE ULTIMATE COMPETITIVE ADVANTAGE